Welcome to the Algarve!

Welcome to the warmth of the Algarve . . . to the friendliness of its people, the splendour of its early-blossoming springs, the delicious laziness of its long summers and the glory of its late autumns.
Here you will delight in clear bright mornings and the bustle of busy markets ... relax in the peace of sandy coves, lulled by the soft swish of Atlantic waves ... stroll along miles of unspoilt beaches, marvelling at the high drama of clifftop and coastline ... travel sleepy country lanes, meeting ambling donkey carts ..., retreat to the cool distant hills, sweet with the scent of pine and eucalyptus ...

PUBLICAÇÕES FRANK COOK, LDA.
PORTUGAL

The Frank Cook Algarve Guide

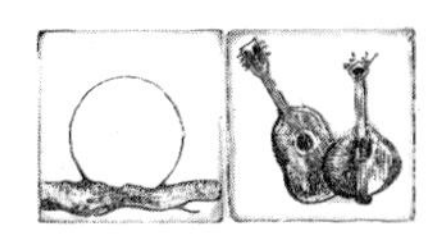

The publishers welcome the comments of readers and users of this guide since we are always trying to improve our publications to help readers enjoy Portugal. Please call us or write to us directly or fill in the questionnaire you will see later in the book. We look forward to hearing from you!

Publicações Frank Cook, Lda.
Rua Saraiva de Carvalho, 32 1200 Lisboa
Portugal
Tel. (01) 601345/677259/650755
Fax. (01) 677275

Series Editors: Christina Hippisley and Paula Fernandes
Assistants: Ana Cristina Santos and Ana Paula Pomar

Photographs:
- Luís and Asta Almeida d'Eça, Lisboa - Tel: (01) 9833041
- Otto Petrie, Karlsrühe, Frankfurt - Tel: (0721) 473514
- Luís Lucas, Grafe Desenho Gráfico e Publicidade, Lda. - Tel: (01) 672379/672495

23.rd edition 1991
ISBN 972-991-17-4

Whilst every care is taken to ensure accuracy the publishers cannot be held responsible for errors resulting from inaccurate information received.

Contents

Special Features

Maps

General Information

Food

Shopping

Algarve property

Sports

Vilar do Golf *(Quinta do Lago)*

Vilar do Golf is where lifestyle and the game of golf find their finest expression. Set in the heart of Quinta do Lago, Europe's most exclusive leisure resort, Vilar do Golf is the perfect location not only for holidays (throughout the year) but for a free-hold property investment. Many properties have lovely views of the sea, seen through the surrounding pine woods and lush semi-tropical landscaping. Right on your doorstep: 36 of the best golf holes in the world, with **guaranteed start times and a 50% discount on the green fees** to residents and guests. You can also enjoy three swimming pools (one heated). The superlative Belvedere Restaurant. And the entire 1700 acre estate of Quinta do Lago, fringed by golden sandy beaches and the warm Atlantic.

Vilar do Golf is owned and managed by Trafalgar House Europe, a member of the Group whose assets include the QE2 and the Ritz Hotel.

For more information, please contact: Vilar do Golf, Quinta do Lago, 8135 Almansil, Algarve, Portugal. Tel: (089) 396647. Fax: (089) 396695, or call the U.K. Sales Office on (0272) 240867.

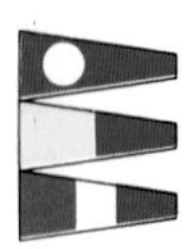

TRAFALGAR HOUSE EUROPE

Algarve

Cities, Towns and Villages

The contents of this book are arranged in the following order:

Pages 6-42 Special features of the Algarve. See page 3.

Pages 55-127 Cities, towns and villages. See below. In this section Faro airport is taken as the starting point from which one travels first westwards to Sagres (pages 65-120) then eastwards to the Spanish border (pages 121-127).

AREA TELEPHONE CODES: **Tavira 081 . Portimão 082 . Faro 089.**

Algarve
— today

The sleepy, quiet Algarve of the 1960s, slowly awakened over the last two decades by its increasing popularity as a prime holiday destination, still remains largely unspoilt. Its local inhabitants continue to be the "friendliest in Europe".

However, the increasing demands for accommodation, hotels, apartments and villas has accelerated expansion in the building industry, sometimes at the expense of more traditional rural occupations.

Local inhabitants, once dependent on fishing and farming for their livelihood, have found other more lucrative jobs that demand different skills.

Meanwhile, farming methods themselves have changed and become more modern. Ox-drawn ploughs and delicate crops left open to the elements are less common. Small tractors, protective plastic sheeting over seedlings, and larger fields are becoming more widespread.

As agriculture changes, so too does local business. Construction, retail shops, tourism-related services and property are all booming industries in the Algarve. Similarly, once quiet towns like Faro, Albufeira, Quarteira, Carvoeiro and Lagos are now humming with activity and new housing for residents and tourists alike.

Not long ago, overdevelopment of this beautiful area seemed inevitable. The lack of a central blueprint to control planning and construction was being felt by tourists and residents alike. Fortunately, the government has stepped in swiftly and now all new construction is strictly controlled within set planning limits, all along the coast from the Spanish border to Sagres at the western end. As soon as current construction projects are completed, the effects of the new legislation will be felt.

Local residents, and visitors, were worried that the mistakes of the Costa del Sol might be repeated in the Algarve. Happily, it seems this will not be the case.

Former "building sites" are settling down and concentrating on their service infrastructures.

Town centres are becoming pedestrianised, beaches are clean and well-equipped, and town landscaping with grass and trees is becoming wide spread.

Algarve
— *today*

The winds of change and control now blowing through the Algarve will help minimise past mistakes and stop the gradual erosion of the area's natural beauty.

Where is it possible, in today's Europe, to walk for miles along beaches washed by the Atlantic? Find a small path leading to a secluded cove for private sunbathing and swimming? See smallholders cultivating crops in centuries-old ways? And where is it possible to have such a wide choice of accommodation - your own villa and pool, or a five star hotel, or a modest self catering apartment?

Here there is something for everyone - especially in the variety of the food, less expensive than other holiday destinations and always fresh, whether its local meat or sea-fresh fish. And don't forget the local handicrafts, tiles, pottery and porcelain, made with the skills handed down through the centuries. There are quality products here, not just the mass — produced usual souvenirs.

The Algarve Tourist Board is the Government entity that promotes the Algarve abroad and in the local area. Its new headquarters in Faro are centralising everything under one roof in a modern building with the latest facilities for lectures and briefings. Built to satisfy the needs of Algarve visitors, the new building reflects the authorities desire to attract quality tourism to the area. **For the latest information on where to go and what to do, contact the Tourist Board's regional offices along the coast.**

Sede/*Headquarters*
Rua Ataíde de Oliveira, 100 — 8000 FARO
Tels: (089) 803667/8/9/70/71 — Telex: 56578 • REGIAL P

POSTOS DE TURISMO/
TOURIST OFFICES

Albufeira
Rua 5 de Outubro
Tels: (089) 512144
Aljezur
Largo do Mercado
Tel: (082) 98229
Armação de Pêra
Avenida Marginal
Tel: (082) 312145
Carvoeiro
Largo da Praia
Tel: (082) 357728
Faro
Rua da Misericórdia, 8-12
Tels: (089) 803667
Lagos
Largo Marquês de Pombal
Tel. (082) 63031
Loulé
Edifício do Castelo
Tel: (089) 414336
Monte Gordo
Avenida Marginal
Tel: (081) 44495
Olhão
Largo da Lagoa
Tel: (089) 713936
Portimão
Largo 1.º de Dezembro
Tels: (082) 23695
Praia da Rocha
Av. Marginal
Tel: (082) 222 90
Quarteira
Avenida Infante Sagres
Tel. (089) 312217
Silves
Rua 25 de Abril
Tel. (082) 42255
Tavira
Praça da República
Tel: (081) 22511
Vila Real de Santo António
Posto de Turismo
Tel: (081) 44495
Faro-Airport
Posto de Turismo
Tel: (089) 822582
Sagres
Posto de Turismo do
Promontório de Sagres
Tel: (082) 64125

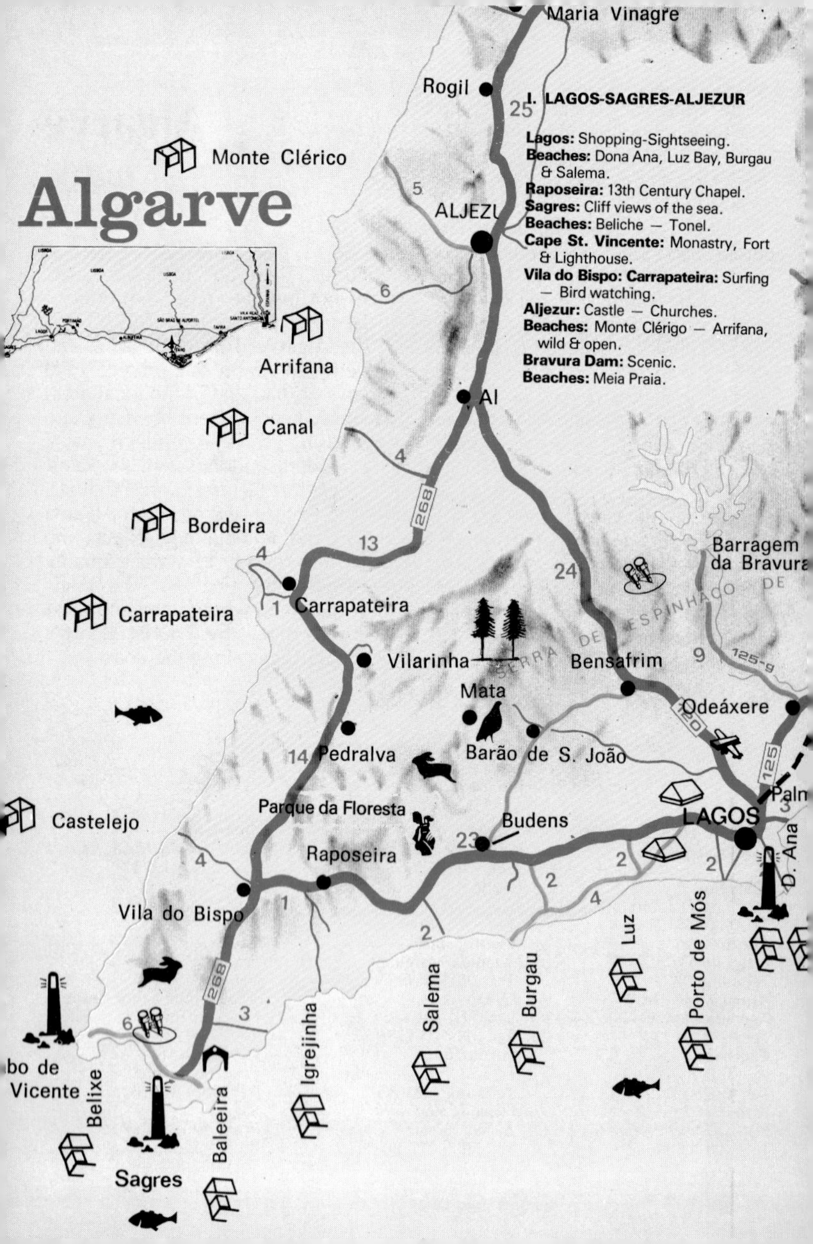

Algarve
Maria Vinagre
Rogil
I. LAGOS-SAGRES-ALJEZUR
Lagos: Shopping-Sightseeing.
Beaches: Dona Ana, Luz Bay, Burgau & Salema.
Raposeira: 13th Century Chapel.
Sagres: Cliff views of the sea.
Beaches: Beliche — Tonel.
Cape St. Vincente: Monastry, Fort & Lighthouse.
Vila do Bispo: Carrapateira: Surfing — Bird watching.
Aljezur: Castle — Churches.
Beaches: Monte Clérigo — Arrifana, wild & open.
Bravura Dam: Scenic.
Beaches: Meia Praia.
Monte Clérico
ALJEZU
Arrifana
Canal
Bordeira
Carrapateira
Vilarinha
Barragem da Bravura
Serra de Espinhaço de
Bensafrim
Odeáxere
Mata
Barão de S. João
Pedralva
Parque da Floresta
Castelejo
Budens
LAGOS
Raposeira
Vila do Bispo
D. Ana
Luz
Porto de Mós
Salema
Burgau
Igrejinha
Baleeira
Belixe
Sagres
bo de Vicente

II. PORTIMÃO-SILVES-MONCHIQUE
Portimão: Shopping — Sightseeing.
Lagoa: Lagoa winery.
Carvoeiro: Beaches; Carvoeiro — Algar Seco.
Silves: Castle, Gothic Cathedral (13th Cent.) Cross of Portugal (16th Cent.) **Arade Dam:** water skiing — scenic. **Caldas de Monchique:** Spa. **Monchique:** Parish Church. **Fóia:** finest view of Algarve. **Ferragudo:** fishing village, castle, beach. **Praia da Rocha:** Fort St. Caterine.
Beaches: Praia da Rocha, Vau, Três Irmãos, Alvor.
LISBOA
LISBOA
ALJUSTREL
DE
SERRA DE MONCHIQUE
Alferce
MONCHIQUE
Montinho de Monchique
Caldas de Monchique
Ribeira de Odelouca
Vale Figueira
SÃO BARTOLO
DE MESSINES
Barragem do Arade
Ribeira do Arade
Calvos
a do Verde
Fonte Louzeira
Porto de Lagos
SILVES
Algoz
Fazenda Caravela
Penina
Tunes
PORTIMÃO
LAGOA
Alcantarilha
Guia
Porches
Ferreir
Pêra
ALBUFEIRA
Três Irmãos
Prainha
Vau
Praia da Rocha
Ferragudo
Rocha Brava
Carvoeiro
Algar Seco
Alfranzinha
Sr.ª da Rocha
Gaivotas
Armação de Pêra
Galé
Castelo
São Rafael
Baleeira
Albufeira
Oura
266
267
266-3
124
269
125
264
270

ALJUSTREL-LISBOA
III. ALBUFEIRA-ALTE-LOULÉ
Albufeira: Shopping — Sightseeing.
Pêra: Scenic valley drive.
Armação de Pêra: Fine beach & Grottoz. Alcantarilha: Ferreiras: Purgatório: Paderne: Alte: are all interesting villages. Salir: Loulé: Sightseeing — shopping.
Almansil: Quinta do Lago, Ocean Club, Vale do Lobo: interesting property developments. Quarteira: Vilamoura: Property development, excellent Marina. Beaches: Falésia, Olhos de Água, Praia da Oura.
Ameixial
Cortes de Ouro
Cachopo
Feitaria
Cortinhola
Alte
Salir
Barranco Velho
Aldeia da Tor
Querença
Almargens
LOULÉ
Peral
Sta. Bárbara de Nexe
Estoi
Milreu
Almansil
Vilamoura
São Lourenço
Vale do Lobo
Pechão
Quinta do Lago
FARO
Cabo de Sta. Maria
Falésia
Açoteias
Vilamoura Marina
Quarteira
Vale do Lobo
Vale do Lobo 2
Lake Sports
Praia de Faro

ALJUSTREL-LISBOA
Ameixial
Cortes de Ouro
Vaqueir
SERRA DO MALHÃO
Cachopo
Feitaria
SERRA DO CALDEIRÃO
Cortinhola
Salir
Barranco Velho
Aldeia da Tor
Querença
Ribeira da Asseca
Almargens
Santa Catarina
LOULÉ
SÃO BRÁS DE ALPORTEL
Peral
Sta. Bárbara de Nexe
Estoi
Milreu
Moncarapacho
Almansil
São Lourenço
Monte do Casal
Vale do Lobo
Pechão
Quinta do Lago
FARO
OLHÃO
Cabo de Sta. Maria
Vale do Lobo
Vale do Lobo 2
Praia de Faro
Ilha da Armona
Fuzeta

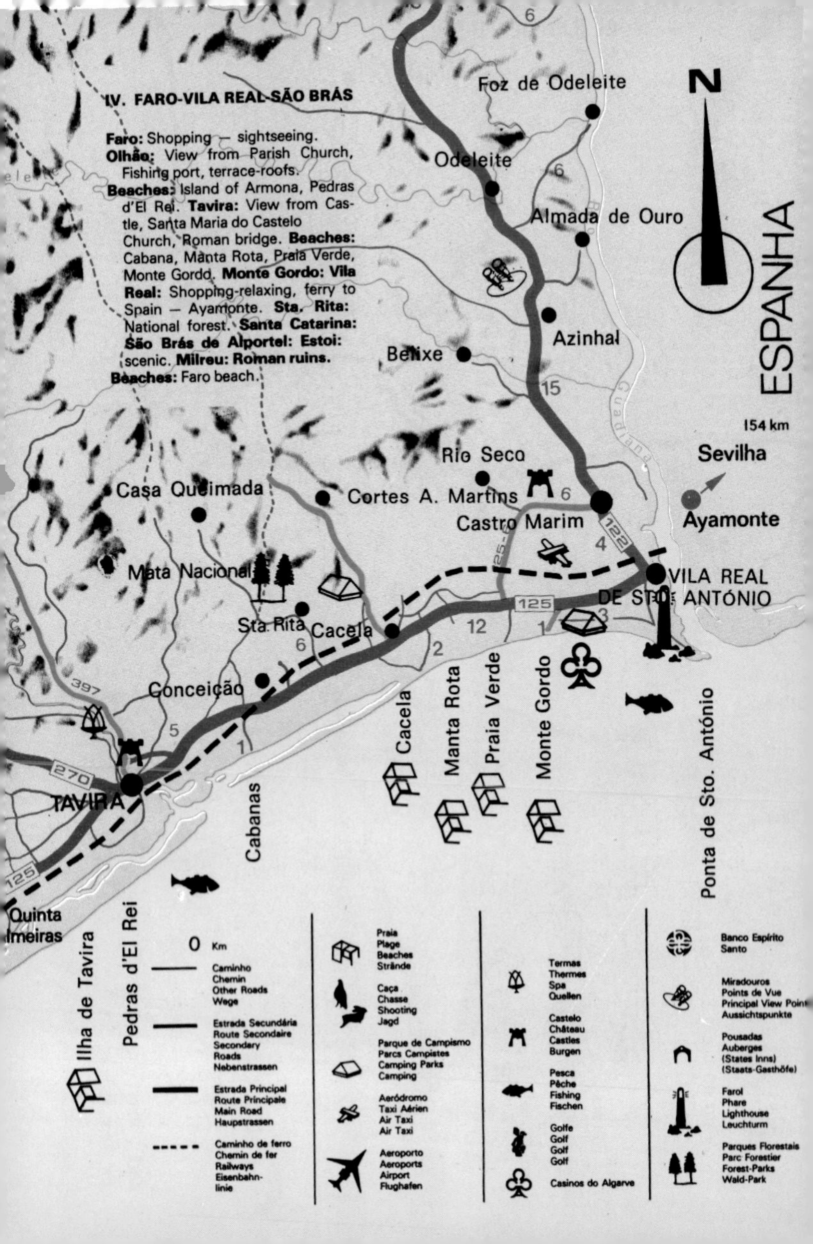

IV. FARO-VILA REAL-SÃO BRÁS
Faro: Shopping — sightseeing.
Olhão: View from Parish Church, Fishing port, terrace-roofs.
Beaches: Island of Armona, Pedras d'El Rei. Tavira: View from Castle, Santa Maria do Castelo Church, Roman bridge. Beaches: Cabana, Manta Rota, Praia Verde, Monte Gordo. Monte Gordo: Vila Real: Shopping-relaxing, ferry to Spain — Ayamonte. Sta. Rita: National forest. Santa Catarina: São Brás de Alportel: Estoi: scenic. Milreu: Roman ruins.
Beaches: Faro beach.
N
ESPANHA
Foz de Odeleite
Odeleite
Almada de Ouro
Azinhal
Belixe
15
Rio Seco
Cortes A. Martins
Casa Queimada
Castro Marim
Sevilha
154 km
Ayamonte
VILA REAL DE STO ANTÓNIO
122
125
Mata Nacional
Sta Rita
Cacela
Conceição
397
270
TAVIRA
125
Quinta
lmeiras
Cabanas
Cacela
Manta Rota
Praia Verde
Monte Gordo
Ponta de Sto. António
Ilha de Tavira
Pedras d'El Rei
0 Km
Caminho
Chemin
Other Roads
Wege
Estrada Secundária
Route Secondaire
Secondary Roads
Nebenstrassen
Estrada Principal
Route Principale
Main Road
Haupstrassen
Caminho de ferro
Chemin de fer
Railways
Eisenbahnlinie
Praia
Plage
Beaches
Strände
Caça
Chasse
Shooting
Jagd
Parque de Campismo
Parcs Campistes
Camping Parks
Camping
Aeródromo
Taxi Aérien
Air Taxi
Air Taxi
Aeroporto
Aeroports
Airport
Flughafen
Termas
Thermes
Spa
Quellen
Castelo
Château
Castles
Burgen
Pesca
Pêche
Fishing
Fischen
Golfe
Golf
Golf
Golf
Casinos do Algarve
Banco Espírito Santo
Miradouros
Points de Vue
Principal View Point
Aussichtspunkte
Pousadas
Auberges
(States Inns)
(Staats-Gasthöfe)
Farol
Phare
Lighthouse
Leuchturm
Parques Florestais
Parc Forestier
Forest-Parks
Wald-Park

Algarve
—its history

Algarve. The very name has a hint of mystery about it. An indication that it is a kingdom of dreams. A land of shadows. It comes from the Arabic 'el gharb' which means the west of 'the land beyond'. Like the rest of the southern Iberian peninsula it bears the unmistakable marks left by 500 years of Moorish domination. Not only in Arabic place names like Alfambra, Faro or Bensafrim, but in its architecture and - most important - in the characteristics of its people. It was in 711 AD that the Moorish invaders swept into the Algarve, but for all their subsequent impact they were by no means the first to colonise the region. The Cynetes first inhabited the southern strip of coast, having come to it from Andalusia. The Phoenicians and Carthaginians established fishing colonies and the ancient Greeks, in their turn, visited the coast. It was, however, the bustling Romans who 'organised' the region, establishing a proper irrigation system, putting agriculture on a properly planned basis and establishing minor cities in their distinctive style. But once the initial challenge had passed they departed and left the region to the Visigoths who occupied it early in the fifth century. It was their occupation that was interrupted by the Moors.

The capital city of this Moorish empire was Chelb, known today as Silves. At the height of its power, it was a river port with direct access to the sea, larger and vastly more important than Lisbon. Its public buildings were elegantly styled and in its gardens artists, writers and philosophers sharpened their wits in learned discourse. In that distant heyday, the city's population topped 30,000 but its value as a port diminished with the silting of the river Arade.

When Silves fell, so fell the empire of the Moors. That dramatic turning point in history came in 1189 when Dom Sancho I, King of Portugal, persuaded German and English crusaders to join him in an attack on the Moors, and the combined army laid seige to Silves. It lasted from mid-July until the beginning of September in that year and resulted in the surrender of the city. And with the fall of Silves the Moorish empire began its inexorable decline.

Though Faro and part of the coastline remained under Moorish domination for another sixty years, the fall of Silves marked the end of an era. From that time the rulers of Portugal called themselves "Kings of Portugal and the Algarve", unconsciously emphasising the region's separate identity.

The Algarve came to real prominence in the fifteenth century, when Prince Henry the Navigator established his school of navigation at Sagres.

It was he who despatched his captains on their monumental voyages of discovery. In the course of a single century Portugal discovered and explored nearly two-thirds of the inhabited globe. The country's contribution to man's knowledge of his planet stands unequalled and it is one of the sad ironies of history that Henry himself died in 1460, before the greatest of those discoveries - before da Gama and Magellan, Cabral and Dias.

Until the fifteenth century the Algarve was almost totally isolated from the rest of Europe - indeed, from the rest of Portugal - and though the activities of Prince Henry did help in some measure to break this isolation, it still remained very much 'the land beyond'. Cut off from the north by the Caldeirão and Monchique mountains and separated from Spain by the Guadiana river it developed in its own way and at its own pace. Although the barriers are now down, the Algarve retains that distinctive character. New highways bring visitors more easily from Lisbon and from other parts of Europe. The airport at Faro is now a firmly established port of entry for jet passengers. Yet despite the proliferation of foreign-registered cars upon the improved roads of the region, despite the development of villas, apartments and hotels, despite the aircraft bringing in their tourist loads, the magic and the spirit of the past prevail.

South of those mountain ranges lies one of the most exciting and unspoiled coastlines in the world. From the frontier town of Villa Real de Santo António, just a ferry ride across the river from Spain, to the sombre greatness of noble Cape St. Vincent, the Algarve stretches for something like 150 kilometres along the south of Portugal.

The Atlantic tide washes its beaches clean and surges constantly around the cape on which Henry established his navigation school. The cape that has been so aptly described as 'o fim do mundo' -'the end of the world'. Along its gentler stretches the rich earth rises red from golden beaches, and twisted rocks shaped by numberless tides scatter the shoreline. It is an area of colour and contrast, rich in agricultural produce, where at certain seasons the almond blossoms dazzle the eye. That white array begins the year, for spring comes in January. As the months unfold beneath the sun, lemons, oranges, carobs, pomegranates and figs grow heavily ripe. Unfamiliar and beautiful flowers dazzle and assault the senses with colour and perfume. Although tourism has had an impact on the region's way of life, every coastal village and town devotes itself to fishing, for it is still a major industry. At night the bobbing lanterns of fishing fleets are a familiar part of the scene, and the types of fish are as numerous as the methods by which they are prepared for the table: mullet, sardine, swordfish, razorfish, tunny, turbot, cod, crab, lobster and clam to name but a few.

The inhabitants of the Algarve share a trait of character with fisherfolk the world over - a steadfastness, a courage and an aptitude for calmly philosophising that is both unique and attractive. But they have other ingredients in their personalities which cannot fail to impress themselves upon the visitor like spontaneous friendship and an almost overwhelming generosity. Their Moorish ancestry can often be detected in lean and alert faces with dark and piercing eyes. Generally dressed in black, the older generation are a dramatic contrast to their surroundings, but many villagers embroider their dresses with flowers or wear one tucked in the brim of their hats. Above all, they possess an unaffected dignity. The younger generation have inevitably altered their personal appearance under the influence of the tourist influx, but though at first sight they seem completely 'European' in their style, the true Algarve character is close to the surface.

A hardworking race, the Portuguese relax with music and dancing. In the Algarve these folk dances are as distinctive as the people, reflecting their mixed history. The music, the 'Corridinho' played on a type of accordion, is fast and strident with an extremely catchy rhythm, even for the uninitiated. On feast days, when the villages have their fairs, everybody is expected to join in the gay whirling dances in the streets and squares, with flowers used for ammunition! The pure fun and gaiety of a feast day in the Algarve is something to see and appreciate. These are the days to buy the local wares and some advice about the most important of activities - shopping for souvenirs - is given in a special section of this guide. But on the general subject of shopping, try to visit at least one of the markets where the local country people auction off farm animals and trade in all types of goods. It is a quite unforgettable and unique experience.

Those who dwell in the Algarve are as devoutly Catholic as their fellow country-men, and the thought of a religious festival without dances, singing, fireworks and processions would be incredible to them. If a visitor is fortunate enough to be in the right place at the right time he will be impressed by the decorations with which the whole festive village is adorned. He will be moved, too, by the contrast between the irresistable, almost childish excitement and the villagers' intense piety.

The climate. The temperature in the Algarve can be as delightful in November as in the height of summer. During the hottest period of the year the sun is tempered by the refreshing Atlantic breezes, but even so the very fair skinned should exercise caution in acquiring a tan. The winter temperature of the sea rarely falls below 59°F. Though the climate is delightful throughout the year, its effect is best appreciated in the early spring, for then the region is an explosion of colours and warmth, blue skies, bright refreshing seas and an abundance of flowers and blossoms. The figures for air and sea temperatures, rainfall and hours of sunshine compare most favourably with other coastal resorts in the world, and the Algarve also enjoys the advantage of a south-facing coastline.

	TEMPERATURE °F		RAINFALL IN INCHES		HOURS OF SUNSHINE
	Winter	Summer	Winter	Summer	
Algarve	50-68	68-86	10-20	5-	Over 3000 hours
Costa Brava	32-50	68-86	5-10	10-20	2000-3000 hours
Majorca	58-68	68-86	5-10	10-15	2000-3000 hours
Adriatic	32-50	68-86	5-10	10-20	1000-3000 hours
French Riviera	32-50	68-86	5-10	10-20	2000-3000 hours
Corsica	32-50	50-86	10-20	8-10	2000-3000 hours
North Africa	50-68	68-86	10-40	5-10	Over 3000 hours
California USA	50-68	68-86	5-	8-10	1000-2000 hours

Language. Those who are unfamiliar with Portugal believe that its geographical proximity to Spain will have resulted in a similarity of language. Nothing could be further from the truth and the distinct language of Portugal is difficult to master. However, one should not have much difficulty picking up a few words and phrases, and local people appreciate when such an effort is made. Please see pages 133-134.

Money and prices. The monetary units are the centavo and escudo (100 centavos = 1 escudo). Confusingly the sign for escudo is the same as for the dollar ($) but is written after the escudo figure and before the centavo. Thus, fifteen escudos and ten centavos is expressed as 15$10. Until this is understood all price lists can be very misleading. Money is best changed in banks, as a more favourable rate is obtained than in hotels.

Transportation. TAP flies regularly from Faro airport to over 50 destinations in 4 continents. During the holiday seasons, a number of specially chartered flights are also arranged. In addition there are daily rail services from Lisbon, including a de luxe express service. (Ferry boat from Terreiro do Paço to Barreiro and from there by train.) There are daily coach services from the Algarve to Lisbon, taking around five hours. Selfdrive or chauffeur driven cars may be hired in Lisbon and the journey to the Algarve takes three or four hours. The following are the distances between Lisbon and the more important centres of the Algarve:

Lisbon - Sagres .... 279 kms
Lisbon - Praia da Rocha ...... 283 kms
Lisbon - Albufeira .... 285 kms
Lisbon - Faro .... 282 kms
Lisbon - Monte Gordo .... 305 kms

Local public transport by train or bus is available and, though services can be slow and infrequent, this is an interesting way to see some of the region. Schedules are available from tourist offices or hotel porters. International and local car hire companies also operate along the Algarve and details are given in the Transport section of the guide's text.

Places to see. Between Cape St. Vincent and Vila Real da Santo António there are dozens of fishing villages and small inland towns whose public buildings, churches and domestic architecture reflect their varied histories. There are lovely drives to be taken through the countryside and staggering views of seemingly endless beaches, broken up by the secluded coves that emerge at every turning of the road. For tour suggestions of which most can be done by organised bus tours, please see pages 7-11 for details and a map of the Algarve.

Places to stay. Though it has come relatively late into the area of popular tourism, the Algarve can provide all kinds of accommodation, from luxury hotels which match the finest in Europe to the simplest of boarding houses, from State built Pousadas (small hotels) to villas and apartments. It also has excellent facilities for those tourists who wish to cater for themselves in camp sites or modest apartments. Detailed information about accommodation in the Algarve may be had from the National Tourist Office, in Praça dos Restauradores, Lisbon, the

Portuguese Tourist offices abroad and along the coast.(see page 7).

Tourist Information. There are government tourist offices located all along the coastal area, staffed with bi-lingual receptionists. Here colourful and informative travel folders are available for the asking along with maps and sightseeing information. Visas are not necessary for American and EEC visitors - on arrival such visitors are given a passport stamp valid for two months at no charge. This may be extended by simply presenting the passport to the proper office, which can be arranged through a hotel porter. The Portuguese will generally go out of their way to please visitors, and are renowned for being *"the friendliest people in Europe"*. When asking for directions, for example, do not be surprised if your informant takes you part of the way in order to make sure you are heading correctly!

Tipping. All hotel, bar, restaurant and other tourist charges include a service charge. An additional tip usually depends on the quality of service. A point to remember in restaurants is that service can be slow, the Portuguese taking the sensible attitude that holiday makers should be relaxing and that a good meal is not to be rushed.

Wining and dining. Most of the larger villages and towns have restaurants and night clubs, discotheques and 'boites' which are independent of the hotels. The emphasis of food in the Algarve is, not surprisingly, on fish. Even the most experienced gourmet is likely to be pleasantly surprised by the excellence and infinite variety of his meals. It has been claimed by many visitors that grilled sardines eaten in some modest beach bar or in simple restaurants near a town's market are unsurpassed, even though the gastronomic trimmings may be absent. The larger hotels pride themselves on their restaurants, though in these the emphasis tends to be on an international cuisine. The visitor should not hesitate to explore and sample the small restaurants in towns and villages. A guide to some of the better known local dishes is to be found on page 19.

Apart from the traditional Portuguese table wines, ports and brandies, the Algarve produces its own wines, mainly from the Lagos area. An unusual brandy, which should be tried, is the aguardente de **medronho** *(see also pages 18 and 19)*.

Night Life. The night clubs, discoteques and 'boites' run the gauntlet in decor, sophistication, simplicity, gaiety and out and out 'swinging'. A number have been grafted on to the local scene, reflecting the nationalities of their owners (as have some of the restaurants), and aiming their attraction at visitors from particular foreign countries.

Fado singing, one of the great traditions of Portugal, is heard increasingly along the Algarve, and there are some folk dance groups performing at hotels. For very many visitors, however, the best form of evening relaxation is to sit outside a cafe on a warm evening, sipping wine and watching the world go by.

There is **gambling** and **nightly entertainment** at the **Alvor, Monte Gordo and Vilamoura Casinos.**

PORTUGUESE FOOD

The cuisine of the Algarve is distinctive and varied and is as worthy of exploration as the region itself. The simplest introduction to it is, perhaps, **Sardinha Assada** - fresh grilled sardines eaten straight from the charcoal grill with a salad and washed down with a strong red wine. Of the soups, **Caldo Verde** is regularly found on restaurant menus, being a simple potato soup with finely shredded green cabbage. **Caldeirada** is another name to watch out for, a chowder of several species of fish, shellfish, potatoes and tomatoes, flavoured with onion, garlic, malagueta and pimento. **Cataplana** is the name of a special dish in which clams and meat are cooked together - a double pan which has been likened to a primitive pressure cooker.

Algarve is famous for its rich cakes and sweetmeats, many of which must be of Arab origin. The principal ingredients are eggs, sugar and almonds. Some of the names of these sweets: **Bolo Algarvio** (Algarve Cake), **Fios de ovos** (Egg Threads), **Dom Rodrigos** (Something Special) and **Morgado de figos do Algarve** (Fig Sweetmeats).

Algarvian bread is delicious, crusty and very 'more-ish'. It is baked daily (except Sundays) in traditional wood-burning ovens which leaves a fine dusting of ash on the bottom of the loaves. For breakfast fare try 'Papo Seco', a lovely crisp golden roll. 'Pão Caseiro' is a wonderful misshapen mound of a loaf which more than satisfies afternoon and evening hunger pangs, while 'Pão Integral', natural wholemeal bread and rolls with a wholesome and nutty taste is for the health fan.

Portuguese cuisine can be a delight!

The highlight of an Algarvian day is a memorable evening out. Algarvian cuisine encompasses the best of the sea with fresh vegetables, wild game and free range animals roasted with wine in a special oven (o forno). All are a culinary delight! The best way to discover such treats and the wide selection of excellent Portuguese wines, is to ask the owner/ waiter.

For starters, many restaurants have their own carefully guarded recipe for fresh fish soup (Sopa de Peixe). Other starters include the delicate flavour of Smoked Swordfish (Espadarte Fumada) or the slightly salty flavour of steamed fresh shrimp (Camarões Cozidos). Only the most adventurous will discover the wonderful taste of Rock Barnacles (Perceves), a Portuguese favourite. Large Crab (Santola), or Smaller Crab (Sapateira), Large Shrimp (Gambas), in garlic butter or served grilled, or Scampi, (Lagostim) are also excellent starters. All are sold by the kilo (specify the quantity you would like and ask for the corresponding price).

With these temptations the danger is that you will not leave room for the masterpiece ... the dinner! For lovers of fish nothing can surpass the nowadays rare experience of fresh fish so do try something other than the ubiquitous sole. Try some of the Portuguese favourites including: Sea Bass (Robalo), Sea Bream (Besugo), Small Bream (Safio), Big Bream (Cherne) (delicious pan fried), or Monkfish (Tamboril) often served on a kebab. Many say there is nothing better than the traditional Cataplana, a steamed pot of clams, pork, herbs, garlic, onions, tomatoes and white wine (made only to order - preparation takes 45 minutes but well worth the wait). Other favourites include small Stuffed Squid (Lulas Recheadas), or Grilled Tuna Steaks (Atum Grelhado). Cod (Bacalhau) is the most traditional of all dishes.

Bacalhau a Braz - tiny pieces of Cod cooked with tiny fried potatoes and onions is a must! Bacalhau com Grão with Chick peas or Bacalhau à Zé do Pipo cooked with layers of fried onions and mashed potatoes, are some other favourites!

Heartier fare includes spicy Roast Kid (Cabrito no forno), Roast Suckling Pig (Leitão), Roast Veal (Vitela Assada) or Lamb Stew (Ensopado de Borrego). No translation can describe the taste of Feijoada, a piquant Lima bean and meat stew with tomatoes, onions and wine. Febras de Porco are thinly sliced pieces of loin of pork piquant, Porco Alentejana is a garlic dish of cubed loin of pork with cubed fried potatoes, parsley and garlic.

Algarvian desserts include Creme Caramel, Almond Cake and Tarte (Torte or Torta) and Chocolate Mousse (page 17 for others). Of course, in the land of sunshine there is plentiful fresh fruit every day of the year. Starting with January and going through the seasons there are: oranges of every variety, strawberries, melons, cherries, grapes, figs, apples, pears. Or try the delicious cheeses: Camembert, São Jorge, Serra (from the mountains). All traditionally served with bread and quince jelly (marmelada). There is also fresh Goat cheese (Queijo Fresco).

To complete a real feast, try a 'Doce Regional' (local sweet), a speciality of the Algarve, lovingly shaped into delicate birds and flowers. After dinner - Portuguese Brandy (Macieira) or Liqueur is the best way to savour the evening. Liqueurs are made from an old secret formula (Beirão), Almonds (Amendoa Armarga or Amarginha) or Coffee Beans (Tijuana) or Passion fruit (Maracuja). For a real eye-opener, have the firewater (Bagaço or Medronho).

Perhaps nowhere, other than along the 100-mile coastline of the Algarve, is it possible to see such concentrated fishing activity.

The larger boats can be seen daily, heading for the open sea — or returning with their catch to **Vila Real de Santo António, Tavira, Olhão, Faro, Portimão, Lagos** and **Sagres**. At night too, you may see the long line of the fishing boats lanterns bobbing out at sea — giving the appearance of some kind of off-shore street lighting!

Having the advantage of being an open dock area, **Portimão** offers the most colourful scene — with fishing boats, fishermen and open air wooden sheds, where you can be served with delicious freshly grilled sardines, chips and salads, plus of course, the inevitable glass of wine or beer.

The gaily painted open boats returning in the early morning with the previous evening's catch make an exciting and fascinating beach scene... with the fishermen unloading all kinds of fish ... the auctioneers ... and the buyers.

Local markets provide a wealth of noise, bustle and colour which never ceases to fascinate. The main markets are at: **Olhão, Faro, Albufeira, Loulé, Armação de Pêra, Portimão** and **Vila Real de Santo António** and are, in most cases, housed in cool stone buildings. Here you will find butchers, fishmongers and endless stalls selling fresh fruits, vegetables and herbs. Outside in market squares and side streets are numerous pedlars selling clothes, materials, pottery and gift items. Arrive early if you plan to shop as well as sightsee, as many of the best buys — like fresh fish — are soon snapped up by the Portuguese housewives.

Algarve's greatest asset - unlike most Mediterranean resorts - is the abundance of beautiful, clean sandy beaches. An early morning dip or an evening walk along a near-deserted beach in the sunset, is to know the meaning of paradise.

A number of the Algarve's beaches are well organised, offering parking facilities, beach umbrellas, toilets, and often a very good beach restaurant where you can enjoy fresh, charcoal grilled food in the open air. If seclusion, a long hot bask in the sun, a beach picnic and a refreshing bathe are more what you have in mind, then seek out one of the many delightful little sandy coves. Alternatively, you might prefer the unbounded freedom of unspoilt miles of beaches bordered only by colourful cliffs and surf.

Although the beaches of the Algarve are consistently sandy, the cut of the coastline varies considerably. At Sagres, you'll find the cliffs high, stone hard and not a little forbidding - capable as they are of resisting the constant pounding of the waves on the eastern side. However, from Salema to Lagos, Praia da Rocha and on to Albufeira, the cliffs are made mainly of fossil and are thus softer and more subject to erosion from the elements.

Here you will find the lovely coves, caves and grottoes - some accessible only by sea. If you can find an experienced boatman to take you, a trip through the grottoes by boat is an experience not to be missed - but don't try it alone, as the currents are deceptively strong. From Quarteira to the Spanish border you'll see that the cliffs start to change from rich red to a softer ochre colour, as the land comes gently down to meet the sea.

ANNUAL EVENTS

During the year there are dozens of local fairs, exhibitions, sports events and feast days in the Algarve which commemorate the days when it was a simple rural community with its own customs and rituals. Many of these country customs still survive and visitors to the Algarve will enjoy immensely watching or taking part in these events. The Algarve Tourist Board (see page 7) distributes monthly calendars of events which detail the exact time and place of that month's events. Below we indicate the most interesting events that you should try to attend.

Fairs.

Art and Handicraft Fair
June/July Faro
The Tavira Book Fair
late August Tavira Garden
Antique Fair
May-December weekly.
Largo de Sé, Faro
Handicrafts Fair
July, Albufeira
The Food Fair
August, Lagos
Fatacil 1991
16-25 August 1991
Exhibition Park, Lagoa
(One of the highlights of the calendar-handicrafts, food and much more)
Citrus Fair
February/March, Silves
Handicraft Fair
August, Largo de Carmo, Tavira
Agritavira/Agricultural Fair
August, Parque das Feiras,
Horta do Campo, Tavira
Tourist Fair
April, Hotel Almansor,
Praia do Carvoeiro.

Exhibitions.

Traditional Algarve Clothing
February-May
Casa de Cultura António Bentes,
São Brás de Alportel.
São Lourenço Cultural Centre
Aniversary Exhibition,
March-April,
Centro Cultural São Lourenço,
Almansil.

Sports Events.

Almond Blossom International Cross Country Race.
February, Aldeia das Açoteias,
Albufeira
International Carnival Sailing
Tournament.
February, Vilamoura.
Motonáutica/Iberian Grand Prix
(Sailing)
August
Praia da Rocha
Cycling Tour of Algarve
Faro
Algarve Car Rally
October-November

Algarve Portuguese Open
An important Golf tournament on the European Tour.
Transalgarve
March motor rally from Vilamoura all over the Algarve.
Dom Pedro International Triathalon
June, Vilamoura.

Cultural Events.

International Music Festival
April-May-June
Concerts, ballet performances and recitals of high quality are held in various places throughout the Algarve.
Christmas Concert
December, Tavira
Theatre Festival
March, Vila Real Santo António
International Photographic Arts Meeting
October-Algarve, Lisbon, Porto
International Algarve Cinema Festival
May in various cinemas in Algarve
Algarve Choral Festival
November near Lagos
Algarve Flower Arranging Competition
June-December
International Video Festival
October-November

Religious Festivals.

Traditional Burial Procession
March, Santa Casa da Misericordia, Faro
Festival of the Sovereign Mother
April, Loulé

Street Festivals.

Street parties daily during July and August throughout the Algarve
Coimbra Fado singing
August throughout the Algarve

National Folklore Festival
September. Folkdancers from all over Portugal demonstrate their artistry in various parts of the Algarve.
Loulé Carnival
February, Loulé. Famous throughout Portugal for its Lenten procession of floats. A true spectacle.
Estoi Pine Festival
May, Estoi/Faro
Festival of Popular Saints
June, Tavira
All Saints Festival
June, Olhão
Seafood Festival
August, Olhão
Montcarapacho Carnival
February, Montcarapacho
Sea and Sardine Festival
Portimão
Vila Real Santo António Festival
February, V. R. S. António
International Algarve Dog Show
October Aldeia das Açoteias, Albufeira.
Sagres Festival
July, Sagres
Beer Festival
Silves

Boxing Day Barbecue at a Travel Club Upminster Villa

Up country. If you are a beach fan, it is easy to miss seeing some of the loveliest Algarvian countryside, as it really involves a trip inland. Behind the sea and sand are narrow roads winding gently up into the hillsides, eventually reaching the hills of Monchique. On the way you can see carob, olive, orange and lemon trees, as well as the familiar fig and almond. You can travel to a quiet river valley where women wash clothes in the river, as generations have done before. You may be lucky enough to see a turtle basking in the sun. You will see lonely farms, herds of black goats, breathe in the distinctive perfume of the eucalyptus trees and pass under cool, tall pines. Gradually the landscape and the architecture changes and you arrive at the sleepy little spa town of Caldas de Monchique, to relax in the quiet square, then climb higher, maybe stopping to enjoy a delicious chicken piri-piri at an open air restaurant or to buy some pottery or wickerwork. Finally you will reach the summit, where you can admire the glorious view over hillside, valley and plain to the far distant sea. For details of other scenic drives through the countryside see pages 8-12.

For golfers, the Algarve offers a splendid choice of top quality courses — fresh, green, well watered and playable all year round. Indeed, for many the Algarve is becoming the European centre for winter golf holidays, as the weather and the many five star hotels, villas and apartments adjoining the courses make time spent in the area a pleasure for all kinds of players. Since the first Algarve golf course opened in the 1960's, more and more golfers from firstly the United Kingdom and now from America, Canada, Scandinavia, Holland, Germany and Spain are flocking to the Algarve every year, Both tourism and hotel chiefs have recognised that winter golf is the ideal offpeak way to fill hotels and keep the tourism industry operating all year round.

There are currently ten courses operating along the Algarve of which the most recent is the 9 hole par 3 course at Vale do Milho, near Carvoeiro. To ensure continuing success of the Algarve as a golfing destination Golfsul was formed in 1985 to oversee the marketing of the Algarve's golf clubs. Currently its members are Parque de Floresta, Palmares, Penina, Vilamoura I, II and III, Vale de Lobo and Quinta do Lago. Contact them at Golfsul, Clube Nautico, Vilamoura, 8125 Quateira Tel. (089) 313536 Fax (089) 889153.

Several new courses are also in construction all along the coast. Two golf courses will be opening in September 1991 at Carvoeiro. One will be 18 holes long and of championship layout, the other an «executive compact course». Another, Alto Golf, opens in June 1991. It is an 18 hole par 72 course and was designed by the late Henry Cotton. A third, Vilasol, an 18 hole par 72 course near Vilamoura marina, also opens in June 1991.

Existing courses have also been expanded to create challenging golfing complexes of different hole combinations. There are now also several private courses, open (ostensibly) only to residents of the houses on or near the courses. See page 27-30 for a complete list.

There is no doubt that the next few years will see the Algarve's golfing reputation increase tremendously as more courses open, widening the choice for visitors and strengthening the area's claim to be a «golfing paradise».

SAN LORENZO GOLF COURSE

Golf Director: John Pennington
Professionals: Brian Evans, Albano Rodrigues
Course length: 18 Holes

Ladies:	**5171 m**
Men:	**5837 m**
pro's:	**6238 m**

Par	**72**
Course record	**64 Brian Evans (GB)**

A course of Championship Standard, and designed by the American architect **Joe Lee**, this beautiful course lies within the **Quinta do Lago** estate bordering the Ria Formosa estuary, and is now part of Trust House Forte. It is for the use of the nearby 5 star THF hotel, the **Dona Filipa**, whose guests play **free** of charge on its magnificent 18 holes.

Facilities: Excellent practice ground, Club House Bar and nightime restaurant.

Tel: (089) 396522-396534
Telex: 56848
Fax: 394288

QUINTA DO LAGO GOLF CLUB

Golf Manager: Mario Barruncho
Professional: Domingos G. Silva
Course Length: Three 9 holes of:
Course A - 3,137 yards (2,870 m)
Course B - 3,225 yards (2,950 m)
Course C - 3,263 yards (2,895 m)
Course D - 3,480 yards (3,068 m)
All par 36. S.S.S.72

Built on the luxury Quinta do Lago estate this 27 hole Championship Golf Course, with its flexibility to play different 17 hole combinations, was designed by American Bill Mitchell. Although the Portuguese Open is often held here the course can be enjoyed by all levels of golfer and is enhanced by lakes, pines, sandy soil and wild flowers.

Facilities: Excellent practice ground, Club house with bar and restaurant. Almansil.

Tel/(089) 394529/394782.
Telex: 56000 GOLFQL P.
Fax: (089) 394013.

VILAMOURA GOLF CLUB - Course I

President: Dr. Júlio Baptista Coelho
Marketing Manager: Susete Calado
Course Maintenance: Eng.º Jorge Marcelo
Professional: Joaquim Catarino
Course length: 6,924m Yards (6,331m); 18 holes; Par 73; S.S.S. 72
Course records:
— Amateur: 66 M. Smith (G.B)
— Professional: 67 D. Smith (GB)
Tel: 089-313652 - 889908
Telex: 56914 LUGOLF P.
Designed by Frank Pennink the course is set on elevated ground with narrow fairways carved through umbrella pines.

VILAMOURA GOLF CLUB - Course II

President: Dr. Júlio Baptista Coelho
Marketing Manager: Susete Calado
Course Maintenance: Eng.º Jorge Marcelo
Professional: Joaquim Catarino
Course length: 6,256 m 18 holes; Par 72 - S.S.S. 71
Championship: 6,256m Men: 5,866m Ladies: 5,225m
Course record:
Professional: 69 Peggy Conley (GB).
Tel: 089-315562/312704
Telex: 56018 VIGOLF P.
Frank Pennink also designed this fairly flat course with a beautiful sea view. The new holes designed by Trent Jones introduce a fine contrast to attract and appeal to all levels of players.

FACILITIES ON BOTH COURSES: Club hire, club repairs, trollies, buggies, putting greens, practice ground, lessons by professionals, well stocked pro-shops, golf museum (Vilamoura I), bars and restaurants right on the practice tee. (Vilamoura II).

VILAMOURA GOLF CLUB Course III:

True american style course designed by the famous architect Joseph Lee (USA). 27 challenging holes set up along the coast, among 10 different small lakes.

VALE DE LOBO GOLF CLUB

Golf Secretary: Mrs Janet Walker
Professional: Stephen Walker.
Three 9 hole courses: Yellow 3,036 metres, Par 36; Orange 2,975 metres, Par 36; Green 2,753 metres, Par 35; Course records: Amateur 72 on Yellow and Orange courses - T. Koch de Gooryndd. Professional 64 on Green and Orange courses - Brian Evans. Tel: Faro (089) 394444

Green Fees: Daily (special rates for Vale do Lobo guests and property owners). **For Hire:** Clubs, golf carts and trolleys. Excellent practice range. Clubhouse with restaurant, bar, pro-shop and changing rooms.

VALE DO MILHO GOLF CLUB

Golf Secretary Susan Hart
A 9 hole par 3 course designed by former Ryder Cup player David Thomas.
970 metres long.
Tel 082 358502 - Fax 082 358497
Telex 577441 JLGOLFP
Situated in the midst of the Jorge de Lagos Village and Country Club at Carvoeiro. Green fees, call for information.
Facilities: Club Hire, practice putting green, bar.

PENINA GOLF CLUB

Golf Secretary: Leonel Rio.
Championship course: Medal tees 6,889 yards (6,263 metres): maximum 7,450 yards. 18 holes. Par 73. Course records: Professional: 66 V Barrios (Es.) Also two 9 hole courses, the North and Monchique. Penina Golf Hotel. Tel: (082) 415415. Telex: 57307

Green Fees: By arrangement; daily, weekly, fortnightly or monthly. For clients in hotel GOLF GREEN FEE is complementary. Green fees entitle use of king size swimming pool.
For Hire: Caddies, clubs, electric golf carts, trolleys.

PALMARES GOLF CLUB

Director: F. Cabral. Secretary: D. Garvey. Par 71 with three par 5's, eleven par 4's and four par 3's.
Meia Praia - Lagos. Tel: (082) 62953.
Telex: 57434 Palmar P - Caixa Postal 74.
Green Fees: By arrangement, daily, weekly, fortnightly or monthly. **For Hire:** Caddies, clubs, trolleys and golf carts.

PARQUE DA FLORESTA

Designed by "José" Pepe Gancedo.
Golf Director: Thomas Pidd
Course length: 6,492 yards. (5,888 m) 18 holes. (par 72).
Tel: (082) 65333/4/5.
Telex: 57173 GOLSAN
16 kms. West of Lagos, Budens 8650 - Vila do Bispo.
Green Fees: Daily, weekly, fortnightly or monthly.
For Hire: Clubs, trolleys and golf buggies. Visitors welcome.
Facilities: Attractive Algarvian style Clubhouse, good locker rooms, pro-shop, bar and restaurant. Terrace with spectacular view over golf course and sea. Putting green and driving range.

PINE CLIFFS GOLF AND COUNTRY CLUB

This 9 hole course at the Pine Cliffs/ Sheraton Hotel resort near Albufeira is open, but only residents in the luxury properties near the course and guests in the soon to be completed Sheraton Hotel have access to the course. The Honorary President of the course is Nigel Mansell, the British racing driver. For more information telephone 089 501785/7 Fax 089 501795.

COURSES TO OPEN IN 1991

June - Vila Sol Golf Club

This 18 hole par 72 golf course is situated on a picturesque 367 acre site in the rolling pinelands behind the Vilamoura estate. The course is 6183 metres long and English golf architect Donald Steel has designed the greens, rolling fairways, doglegs and lakes to challenge even the most experienced golfer. The course occupies 1/3 of the land, with other land reserved for villa plots. The Vila Sol Golf Club will be run as a private club with membership rights reserved for property owners and their guests. It will have 720 members and 120 non-owner founder members.
For more information contact (089) 301295 Fax (089) 301299 Vila Sol, Alto do Semino, 8125 Algarve.

June - Alto Golf

This 18 hole, par 72 championship course is situated on a majestic site 2 kms from Portimão and overlooking the sea. It was designed by the late Henry Cotton, his last Algarve golf course. It has several demanding holes, including the «Henry Cotton Challenge». The course is an integral part of the Alto Golf development, which will consist of freehold properties around the fairways. Although destined to be a private course for residents and guests in the resort, it will initially be open to the public.
For more information contact (082) 459119

September-Euroactividade

Euroactividade AG will be opening 2 courses in September, after 2 years of construction. One will be 18 holes and of championship standard. The second will be an «executive compact course». The courses are designed by Ronald Freame, the Californian golf course architect, and are situated on 142 hectares of land between Lagoa and Ferragudo, in the centre of the Algarve. Also on offer are 500 building plots, and in principle a golf village with shops and a restaurant.
For more information contact (082) 357266 Telex 57655

For year-round riding through the pines and along sandy paths and beaches, both in sunlight and moonlight, the Algarve is difficult to surpass. Stables dot the coastline and vary from the more sophisticated, with Anglo-Arab and Lusitano horses to ponies for child riders.

Place	Page	No. of Horses Normally	Riding Facilities Indoor	Outdoor	Instruction	Tel.
Alfa Mar	74	2	-	✔	✔	50351
Torralta		8	-	✔	✔	
Quinta dos Amigos	-	30	-	✔	✔	
Vilamoura	51	6	-	✔	✔	314675
Quinta do Lago (Pine Trees)	-	20	-	✔	✔	394368
Alvor Praia Hotel	-	8	-	✔	✔	458901

TENNIS

Tennis has come up in the Algarve in a big way with the opening of **The Roger Taylor Tennis Centre**, one of Europe's top tennis centres situated in the 5 star resort of Vale do Lobo. Facilities include 12 all-weather courts - 6 floodlit for evening matches - a colonnaded clubhouse with comfortable changing rooms, sauna, heated swimming pool, bar and first-class restaurant.

The David Lloyd Tennis Centre at Rocha Brava, Carvoeiro is also beautifully designed and positioned. Ten courts, squash, swimming pool and restaurant.

Other tennis centres are: **Hotel Montechoro Tennis Centre** with 10 courts, the **Carvoeiro Tennis and Squash Club** with 10 courts, **Hotel Dom Pedro Tennis Centre** with 4 courts, **Vilamoura Tennis Centre** with 8 courts and **Luz Bay Club** with 3 courts.

With excellent facilities and weather, the Algarve will no doubt be holding important tennis tournaments throughout the year as well as providing the best of conditions for all tennis enthusiasts.

Roger Taylor Tennis Centre

Place	Page	No. of Courts	Type	Equipment Sale	Equipment Hire	Changing Facilities	Tel.
Alfa Mar	74	16	all weather				501351
Carvoeiro Clube de Ténis *		10	all weather				357847
Hotel Alvor Praia *	106	7	all weather				458900
Hotel Delfim	106	3	all weather				458901
Hotel Dom Pedro	71	3	all weather				889650
Hotel Dona Filipa	66	2	all weather				394141
Hotel Meia Praia	110	8	all weather				60951
Hotel Montechoro *	77	2	all weather				589423
Hotel Penina	108	2	red clay				415415
Hotel Vasco da Gama*	125	4					44321
Jorge de Lagos - -Village and Country Club			all weather				357195
Ocean Club	117	3	all weather				789472
Quinta do Paraíso *		3	all weather				357278
Torralta		2	all weather				
Vale do Lobo		12	all weather				394444
Vilamoura	51	4	all weather				380088

* Floodlit courts

SAILING

For sailing, other than on the open sea there are lagoons along the coast: Faro, Olhão, Tavira and estuaries, Portimão and Vila Real de Santo António.

Place	Page	Type of Boat Available	Instruction	Tel.
Carvoeiro Club		44ft. Yacht	-	357266
Luz Bay Club	115		✔	789538
Sailing Club Lagos		Sailing dinghies	✔	62256
Torralta		Sailing dinghies	-	20462
Vale do Lobo		Sailing dinghies	✔	394444
Vilamoura	51	Sailing dinghies	✔	313933

SNORKELLING-SCUBA DIVING

Algarve offers snorkelers and scuba divers some magnificent dives along the coast — especially towards the western end where the sandstone cliffs and rocky beaches create grottoes and caves, around Praia da Luz and Armação de Pêra. **The Sea Sports Centre at Praia da Luz Tel (082) 789538** offers organised dives and hires all the necessary equipment to customers. Regular dives inspect old wrecks that sank off the coast in the last world wars.

SQUASH

Carvoeiro Club - 2 courts (coaching). Tel: (082) 357266/357262. **Hotel Alfamar**, Praia da Falesia. Tel: (089) 150351. **Quinta da Balaia.** Tel: (089) 586583. **Hotel Montechoro.** Tel: (089) 859423. There are others being built - check with the Tourist Office.

FISHING-COASTAL EXCURSIONS

FISHING

Sagres and Carrapateira (16 kms to the north) and the beaches of Monte dos Clérigos and Arrifana are considered by sportsmen to be the best fishing grounds in Portugal and among the best in Europe. The ideal season for angling is from the beginning of October to mid-January, for there is wind and according to the fishermen, this is when there are better opportunities. **Shore fishing** - Moray Eel, Grey Mullet, Scabbard Fish, Bluefish, Bass, Glaucous Bream and Tope.

Place	Page	Open	Cabin	Special	Tackle	Bait	Guide	Tel.
Luz Bay Club	116	-	-	-	-	-	-	789538
Alvor Praia Hotel	106	✔	✔	-	-	-	-	458900
Torralta		✔	-	-	✔	✔	✔	
Cepemar (Vilamoura)	73	-	✔	✔	✔	✔	✔	25866 312836

COASTAL BOAT EXCURSIONS

Along the coast companies and fishermen hire out boats for daily and hourly excursions. The 300 kms of coast are exciting to see and explore, obviously not all at one time but by areas. From Portimão to Sagres there are dozens of caves and rock formations to visit or pass through. Many boats stop at secluded beaches for a sardine barbecue lunch.

Organised excursions (not too expensive) from: **Vila Real:** Tours up the Guadiana River. **Tavira:** The Pedras d'el Rei holiday resorts have a Saturday cruise. **Quarteira/Vilamoura:** From the Vilamoura Marina a 30 ton motor sailer and motor yachts available for 3 hour trips and longer. **Albufeira:** Excursions by fishing boats and launches. **Armação de Pêra:** Local fishing boats available for visits to local grottoes. **Portimão:** At main dock near city centre arrangements are made for excursions starting 10.00 and back 16.30. Included is a sardine barbecue on a deserted beach. **Lagos:** Here the local fishing boats cruise through the beautiful coves and grottoes. **Sagres:** Day excursions arranged (through Hotel Baleeira) leaving from Baleeira Beach.

Location: Near Quarteira, 10km from Albufeira, 20km from Faro International Airport.
Latitude: 34º+04'.06"N.
Longitude: 08°+07'18"W.
Number of berths - 1000 with power and water supplies.
Communications: VHF
Call signal: - VILAMOURADIO
Calling Channel - 16/62 transferring to
Working Channel - 20 and 62

A whole complex of luxury apartments, hotels and shops are meeting the needs of the most demanding yachtsman and visitor. The friendly atmosphere at the Nautical Club is most inviting! Amenities around the Marina are continually expanding to meet the requirements of its sailing community.

For further information:

MARINA VILAMOURA, 8125 QUARTEIRA. Tel: (089)302925; Telex: 56843 MARINA P - Fax: (089) 302928

Algarve anchorage and harbour facilities

Place	Page	Anchorage	Depth	Pilot	Fuel	Water
Faro	55	✔	2m/7ft.	✔	✔	✔
Lagos	111	✔	1m/4ft.	✔	✔	✔
Portimão	94	✔	4,5m/15ft.	-	✔	✔
Olhão	121	✔	4,5m/15ft.	✔	✔	✔
Sagres	119	✔	4,5m/15ft.	-	✔	✔
Vilamoura	69	✔	4m/10ft.	-	✔	✔
Vila Real	127	✔	4,5m/15ft.	✔	✔	✔

Reference books: Admiralty Publication 1972 NP 67, West Coast of Spain and Portugal Pilot, 'Roteiro da Costa Algarvia'.

WINDSURFING - WATER SKIING

WINDSURFING

Windsurfing has become very popular along the coast due to easy access to the sea, river basins, one or two lakes and reservoirs.

Place	Page	Boards Available	Instruction	Tel.
Hotel Alfamar	74	✔	✔	150351
Hotel Dom João	113	✔	-	459363
Hotel Montechoro	77	At Praia da Oura	-	589423
Luz Bay Club	115	✔	-	789538
Meia-Praia Beach	110	✔	-	769980
Nautical Center		Alvor Complex	-	458900
Quarteira Beach	70	✔	-	-
Quinta Park (on lake)	65	✔	✔	396666
Vale do Lobo Beach		✔	-	394444
Vilamoura Comercial Center of Marina Vilamoura		✔	-	314058

WATER SKIING

Place	Page	Equipment	Instruction	Tel.
Luz Bay Club	116	✔	✔	789538
Torralta		✔	-	-
Vilamoura	51	✔	✔	380088
Vale do Lobo		✔	✔	394444

Whether you visit the Algarve for business purposes or as a holidaymaker, you will surely not want to leave it without some souvenir - a memento of time spent there. Within a day or two of your arrival you will be well aware that the towns have plenty of shops offering much the same kind of souvenir items as can be bought in any other holiday area - dolls and paperweights, ash trays and wooden carvings. If all you seek are a few inexpensive gifts, then such establishments will supply them. But there is more to a souvenir than that range of goods could possibly encompass. A true memento of any region should reflect its special character, the history that has moulded its arts and crafts. It should, ideally, be an extension of the type of goods which are in everyday use. In this respect the Algarve is well served and the next few pages contain some notes on items of particular interest, items you should especially look out for.

Most people are unaware that Portugal, although tiny, has a glorious history and a rich artistic patrimony. Her craftsmen (and women) stand comparison with the best. Leading department stores throughout the Western world feature Portuguese handicraft products, for example, and the country's leisure wear enjoys a high reputation abroad.

Portugal is famous for many fine products. Among the best known are porcelain, high quality gold jewellery, country pottery, pewter ware and special wines and spirits. The following pages give you an taste of what is in store for you in the Algarve!

PORCELAIN

VISTA ALEGRE, one of Portugal's most famous companies, produces the finest handpainted porcelain dinner services, objects d'art and limited editions for collectors, as well as a range of practical day-to-day tableware.
The firm, founded in 1824, has flourished ever since, and is now synonymous with quality and gracious living. Visit Vista Alegre at;
Rua de Santa Isabel, n.º 21 8500 Portimão
Tel. (082) 23885
(see map on pages 98-99).

PORTIMÃO - RUA VASCO DA GAMA - RUA DIREITA

'ATLANTIS' Full Lead Portuguese Crystal. The art of glass making in Portugal traditionally dates from the 15th century. ATLANTIS is proud to follow the tradition of the Portuguese Glass Art, producing some of the finest Full Lead handmade Crystal. Its reputation is based upon its almost unique clarity, freedom from `colour' and flawless purity.

'VISTA ALEGRE' Porcelain have been producing superbly styled designs since 1790. Most sought after by collectors but VISTA ALEGRE prices are as low as their quality is high. See page 96.

For gifts or for the home the variety of quality Portuguese handicrafts to choose from is most inviting. Details on page 96.

COPPER

Portugal, once a province of ancient Rome and known as Lusitania was the home of the original copperware craftsmen, who were renowned for their outstanding workmanship many thousands of years BC. Today, the craftsmen of Aluminia combine the skills of their forefathers with the most modern techniques to produce copperware, which is supplied the world over.

Photograph by courtesy of O AQUÁRIO, Rua Vasco da Gama 41, Portimão. Details page 96.

JEWELLERY

Real value can be found in silver and gold jewellery designed by skilled Portuguese craftsmen. There is a wide selection of their work to choose from. Photograph courtesy of OLIVEIRA'S JOALHEIRO in Portimão, at Praça Visconde Bivar 12-13. See page 99.

LEATHER

Portugal has long been noted for the excellent value of its leather products and quality workmanship has been combined with good design in the manufacture of shoes. Style, too, has made leather bags a popular purchase and a good selection of belts for men and women are also to be found in the region.

Photography courtesy of CHARLES JOURDAN at ST. JAMES, in Portimão, and Albufeira. Details pages 82, 95.

MATEUS ROSÉ.
CITIZEN OF THE WORLD.

MATEUS
PRODUCED AND BOTTLED IN PORTUGAL.

MATEUS ROSÉ

The Vineyards and the Wealth of Portugal.

Portugal is a wine-producing country whose vineyards cover over 350,000 hectares and employ 235,000 rural labourers (about 20% of the country´s active agricultural labour force) through out the year.

The vineyards were not Nature´s gift nor were they created overnight. Rather they are a testimony to the patient work of many generations of traditional craftsmen whose pride and dedication to the vineyards have meant that Portuguese wine is known for its reputation and quality the world over.

Mateus Rosé and Mateus White.

The birthplace of Mateus Rosé, one of the world´s best selling branded wines, is the historic palace depicted on the bottle´s famous label.

This country mansion, a masterpiece of Baroque architecture, dates back to the beginning of the 16th century.

The inspiration behind this world brand leader was Sogrape´s founder Fernando Van-Zeller Guedes. It was he who cleverly combined the picturesque qualities of the palace with an original label and a unique bottle. The wine itself is another inspiration, since its colour and taste pleases lovers of dry and sweet wine alike.

This clever combination of presentation and taste has resulted in a wine whose success lies in its versatility. Mateus Rosé is suitable for any occasion, as proved by the millions of drinkers in over 120 countries who have enjoyed it over the years.

The grapes from which Mateus Rosé is made are carefully selected from the best red grape varieties grown in the north of Portugal.

As with all Sogrape wines, great care is taken at every stage of the production process, from the selection of the vintage to the bottling, thus ensuring that the highest standards of quality are consistently maintained. To achieve the particularly well-balanced, fresh and fruity quality of the wine, a method called "bica aberta" is used, which allows for long fermentation at controlled temperatures.

Mateus Rosé, fresh and light, is an ideal wine for meals and for those special relaxed moments at home, on the beach, with friends or just alone. Mateus Rosé, the world's most famous rosé, is uniquely suitable for any occasion.

SHOPPING

PORTUGUESE WINES.

There is such a wide variety to choose from! At CASCO GARRAFEIRA, Portimão, a specialist shop in all beverages - very spacious, easy to move around in to make your choice from very ample stocks. Their special **Wine Tasting Area** is inviting and most comfortable.

Photography by courtesy of CASCO GARRAFEIRA, Rua João De Deus, 24, Portimão. Details page 95.

DELICATESSENS.

In Portugal, Delicatessens, 'CHARCUTARIA', have recently become more enterprising and better supplied with foreign and a national produce, sausages, cheese, take-away food; wines and a wide selection of foodstuffs. One of the best in the Algarve is CHARCUTARIA BALAIO, in Portimão.

Photography by courtesy of SUPERMARKET ALVORADA, Rua Diogo Gonçalves, 7, Portimão. Details page 95.

SUPERMARKETS

Over the last few years supermarkets have been opening along the coast where it is possible to do most of your shopping under one roof. One supermarket with variety and ample stocks is ALVORADA in Portimão.

Photography by courtesy of SUPERMARKET ALVORADA, Rua Diogo Gonçalves, 7, Portimão. Details page 95.

Algarve Property

INTRODUCTION

After years as an increasingly successful holiday destination, it is natural that the Algarve has become a magnet for the many holiday visitors who, bewitched by the area's charm and beauty, then buy a villa or apartment. Some retire to the Algarve after a successful business is sold and children are grown; others seek to start a new life away from the hustle and strain of a colder climate and a harsher working environment. Still others buy as an investment, to rent out as holiday accommodation, and their main criteria is the quality of the local rental and maintenance services offered. But all of these people have one thing in common; Where to start? How can they find the oases of quality which are so common along the Algarve coast? On the following pages we have isolated several developments which do, in our opinion, represent the best in reputation, quality of construction, rentals and after sales care and management along the Algarve. Most of the developers we have chosen are household names with excellent reputations to maintain.

As you can see, on the maps below and on the following pages we have indicated the location of each of the chosen property resorts along the Algarve coastline. The maps also show principal beaches and towns. Then, on the following pages each resort is described in more detail, together with illustrative photos.

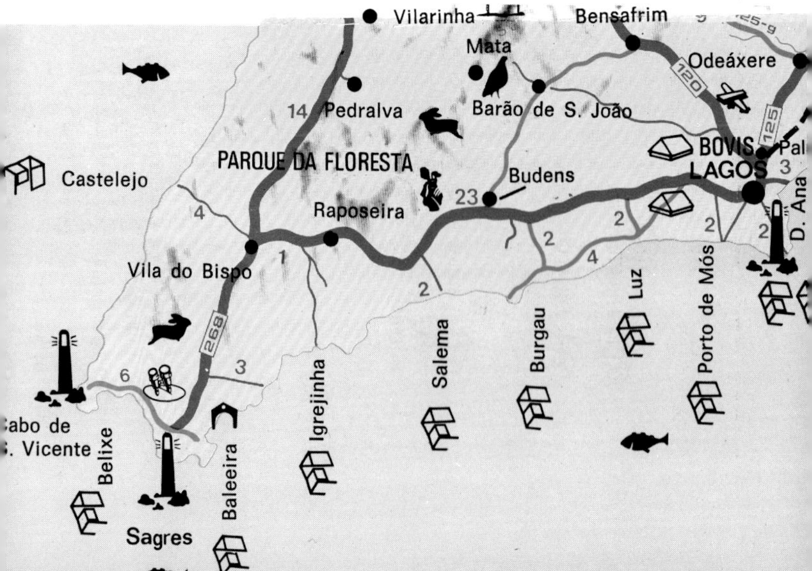

Major Property Resorts

Rocha Brava

Near Carvoeiro lies the spectacular cliff top development of Rocha Brava, owned and managed by Trafalgar House Europe, one of Britain's largest building groups. Within the complex there is a wide range of villas, apartments and sports facilities. See page 47.

São Rafael

A 23-hectare site that overlooks the sea and adjoins two superb sandy beaches. An ideal setting for a truly exceptional complex consisting of villas and village apartments. A full range of amenities includes sports and recreational facilities, restaurants, bars and a supermarket. A world apart yet only 2 kms west of Albufeira and 20 kms from 5 top Golf Courses. See page 48.

Balaia Village

Ten minutes walk from the beach and the lively centre of Albufeira, yet an oasis of peace and calm behind its pines, tennis courts and swimming pools. Balaia Village is a very successful, mature development, now into a further phase of building. It also has a very fine restaurant, A Verandah. See page 49 for more details, and map on p45.

Pine Cliffs Golf and Country Club

Near Albufeira, amidst a dramatic back-drop of sandstone cliffs and umbrella pines, a golf course and residential complex is being built, with a luxury Sheraton hotel at its centre. The whole project is the result of years of planning and environmental considerations. See page 50.

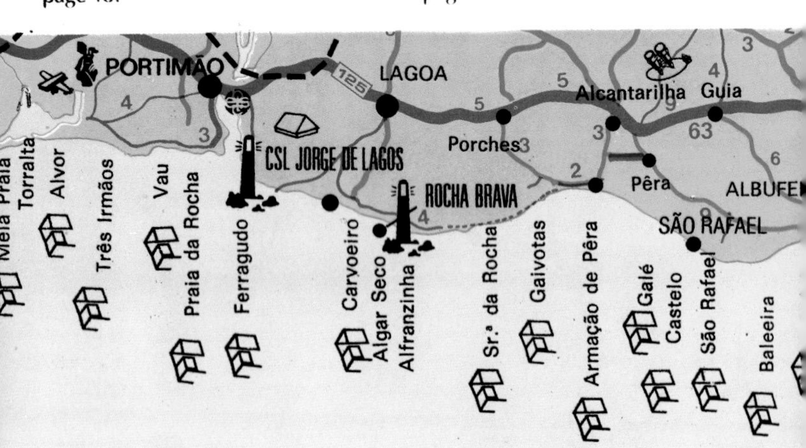

Vilamoura

Is one of the most comprehensive tourist urbanizations ever planned or carried out in Portugal and one of the largest privately developed in Europe. **The Marina Complex** complete with accommodation and all amenities, and its closeness to the Mediterranean, make it an excellent base. Located about 30 minutes from Faro Airport. See page 51.

Vilar do Golf

In the heart of Quinta do Lago, Vilar do Golf, owned and managed by Trafalgar House Europe (also responsible for Rocha Brava) offers freehold properties on the doorstep of a 36 hole championship golf course. See page 4.

Bovis Abroad

This well-known construction company has three property resorts along the Algarve, all offering superb craftsmanship in building. One is near **Lagos**. The other two are within the **Quinta do Lago** estate, offering superb sporting facilities at the championship golfcourses there, and on the lakes near the river estuary. See pages 52-53 for more details.

Boa Vista

Near Tavira, east of Faro and at the quieter eastern end of the Algarve , the Boa Vista development offers individually tailored villas, or high quality apartments.

It offers a chance to invest in an area still tightly controlled by building regulations. See page 54.

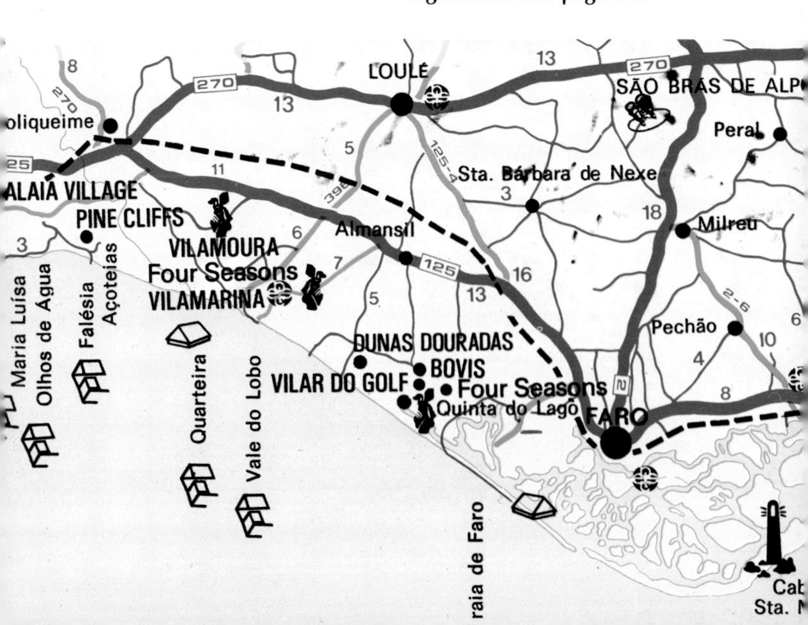

Algarve Property

THE FUTURE.

The government's recent approval of the PROTAL plan for the Algarve has meant fundamental progress for the Algarve property market. The PROTAL plan is the government zoning plan for controlling building in the Algarve, which now, after several years of unwelcome delay, has the force of law behind it. Essentially, the result of the new zoning is to severely restrict new buildings and development in the rural area north of the main EN 125 road, that stretches up into the hills. The western Algarve, from Lagos up to Vila Nova de Milfontes, is now also heavily protected. The effects of this rezoning will be felt throughout the Algarve over the next few years. Within the restricted areas, plots that already have an old building or ruin will be sold at a premium, since rebuilding of these older houses is permitted. Existing newer houses within these areas will also command a better price. All existing projects approved before the new laws were passed are still able to go ahead but have to be started within a certain time frame. This inevitably means more construction over the short term, but of a kind in keeping with the environment and with the necessary infrastructures. Many observers feel that property in the Algarve in general will hold its value better in the future now PROTAL is fully in force.

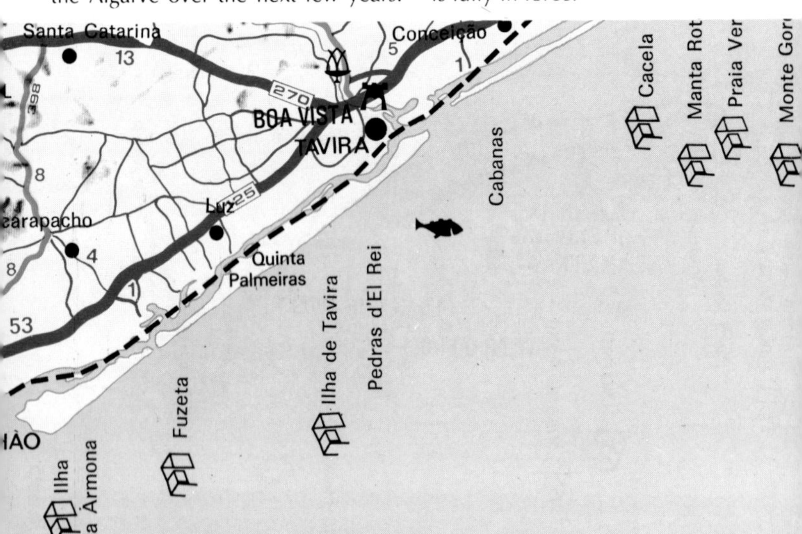

Rocha Brava *(Carvoeiro)*

Rocha Brava basks in the Algarvean sun, high above the warm clean Atlantic Ocean. It is a development of extraordinary beauty, created with all of the style and confidence of Trafalgar House Europe.

Properties range from 1 and 2 bedroom apartments to 2 and 3 bedroom family villas with roof terraces, a limited number of detached villas with private pools are also available. Whatever your choice, the dramatic sea views, the quality of building and reassurance of buying from Trafalgar House, the wonderfully relaxed atmosphere, and superb facilities for loisure and recreation will be - incomparably - the same.

What makes Rocha Brava doubly attractive is the company behind it. Trafalgar House Europe is a member of the world famous Group whose assets include Cunard (the QE2), The Ritz Hotel, and one of Britain's biggest house builders, Ideal Homes.

Prices are from around £73,000 to over £200,000 freehold, or £22,950 for a freehold share in the popular and established Four Owner Scheme.

For further details contact: Rocha Brava, Apartado 47, Praia do Carvoeiro, 8400 Lagoa, (082) 58775/ 9, Telex 574-23 BRAVA P.

Or call the UK Sales Office on (0272) 240867.

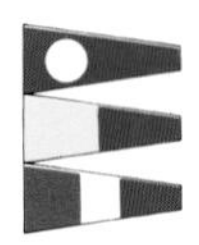

TRAFALGAR HOUSE EUROPE

São Rafael *(São Rafael)*

São Rafael, 'the Magic of S. Rafael' is a splendid property resort overlooking the long sandy beaches near **Albufeira**. No villa or apartment is less than 250 metres from the sea. After 5 1/2 years of operation, many apartments have been completed and these are grouped around a central swimming pool complex, and luxurious restaurant and bar. Flowers and trailing shrubs surround the apartments and pool, adding a tropical exotic touch. About 100 more apartments around a separate swimming pool complex are still being constructed, as are several large detached luxury villas each with over 550 metres of beach frontage. The management anticipates the whole complex will be completed by the early 1990's.

Luckily the current construction hardly disturbs the peace and calm of São Rafael. The staff are very pleasant and try exceptionally hard to make sure visitors enjoy their stay, whether they are freehold owners, co-owners or simply renting a house or apartment for a few days . The resort also offers tennis, windsurfing, a supermarket, 24 hour reception and security, and a bus service to Albufeira and back.

As the remaining apartments are constructed so more services will be provided. More shops, a jacuzzi, snooker, a heated swimming pool and a laundry service will supplement other sports like squash, bowling, croquet, putting greens and more clay tennis courts.

For more information contact São Raphael, Sesmarias, 8200 Albufeira. Tel (089) 591066/591154 Telex 56366/56952 RAPHAEL P Fax (089) 591366.

A utilizar somente
no Continente e
Regiões Autónomas

R S F

BILHETE POSTAL
Resposta
Autorizada pelos CTT

Não carece de selo.
O porte será pago
pelo destinatário

Á

PUBLICAÇÕES FRANK COOK

RUA SARAIVA DE CARVALHO, 32

1200 LISBOA

LUSOPHILES!

The editors of the Frank Cook Travel guides would appreciate your help in improving the books to suit **your** needs. Answer the questionnaire, post this card (free within Portugal) back to us and you will receive free copies of all our annual guides as they are published.

Name ______________________________
Home address ______________________________
______________________________ Tel. ______________________________
Country ____________ Age ______ Job title ______________
What part(s) of Portugal are you visiting?
____

Why did you decide on Portugal? word of mouth ☐
press ☐ own property here ☐ via Portuguese Tourist Office ☐ other (specify) ______________

What will you do while you're here?
sightseeing ☐ shopping ☐ inspecting/buying property ☐
eating out ☐ driving ☐ golf ☐ other (specify) ______________

How long are you staying? ______________

Are you a frequent visitor to Portugal? Yes ☐ No ☐
2/4/6 times a year? ______________

Is your trip planned by
incentive organisers? Yes ☐ No ☐ Which company? ______________
travel agent? Yes ☐ No ☐ Which? ______________
Tour operator? Yes ☐ No ☐ Which? ______________
yourselves? Yes ☐ No ☐ ______________

Are you staying in
self catering? Yes ☐ No ☐ Which? ______________
Hotel? Yes ☐ No ☐ Which? ______________
Private villa? Yes ☐ No ☐ Which? ______________

Which airline did you arrive on? ______________
Will you hire a car? ______________
How did you receive our guide? ______________
Bought abroad ☐ Bought in Portugal ☐
Portuguese Tourist Office ☐ Trade fair ☐
property agents/developers ☐ airline ☐
other ☐ Which? ______________

How could we improve the Frank Cook guide? ______________
____

Would you like more information on our range of maps ☐
videos ☐ and guides ☐ to Portugal? ______________

General comments ______________
____

ALGARVE/91

Balaia Village *(Balaia)*

In the heart of Algarve lies Balaia Village. The project is laid out among mature pine, cork and olive trees. A perfect natural setting for the villas and apartments designed in the traditional style of the Algarve. Integrated in its grounds are magnificent swimming pools for summer and winter use, with separate pools for young children. Tennis courts and a 50 base golf driving range with putting green and bunkers under the direction of a golf pro are available for the more energetic, whilst a short walk of some 300 meters leads to the beautiful Algarve coast, where the ocean laps two marvellous sandy beaches. For golfers, Vilamoura, with its three championship courses is a 10 minute drive. The shopping and nightlife of Albufeira and Montechoro are within similar travelling time. Make sure you visit "A VARANDA", Balaia Village's poolside restaurant, where an innovative chef has already attracted much praise. Reservations in advance are advisable. Moreover, Balaia Village is an associate development of award winning Prowting Homes, the U.K. housebuilding group; another reason why Balaia Village is so sucessful.

For more information contact:
Balaia Village; Balaia, 8200 Albufeira, Tel: (089) 501271 - 501754 - Fax: (089) 501265
Restaurante "A Varanda": Tel: (089) 501271/3
English agent:
Longcroft Properties Ltd. 12, St. Giles Barton Hillesley Wotton-Under-Edge Gloucestershire GL12 8RG ENGLAND Telefone: (0453) 521054 Telefax: (0453) 521058

Pine Cliffs (Açoteias)

At **Pine Cliffs Golf and Country Club** you could wake up to a view like this every morning.

Overlooking spectacular ravines above a stretch of secluded beach, Pine Cliffs is designed and built to the highest specifications and is the result of three years of research, development and detailed planning. Easily accessible, the resort is only half an hour's drive from Faro airport.

The village centre is surrounded by a limited number of villas, town houses and apartments and features the unique five star **Sheraton Hotel**. Constructed in a traditional style of Portuguese architecture, only three storeys high, it comprises luxury suites, boutiques, restaurants and bars, sun terraces and a 25-metre 'indoor-outdoor' swimming pool for use all the year round.

The club has a wide range of amenities including a par 32 nine hole golf course which is exciting and challenging to the novice and experienced golfer alike, tennis and squash, health and fitness centre, beach club and watersports.

Pine Cliffs Golf and Country Club will guarantee complete privacy-sports and hotel facilities are provided for the exclusive use of residents and guests only. Access is via a single entrance and exit, manned 24 hours a day.

Sales of real estate in the resort are progressing rapidly. The first purchasers have now taken possession of their properties and are enjoying the superb facilities.

To arrange a convenient appointment for your private viewing please call or write to our director of sales at Pine Cliffs Golf and Country Club, PO BOX 246, Almansil 8135, Portugal. Tel: (089) 50785/7, Fax: (089) 50795 Telex: 58524.

Vilamoura *(Vilamoura)*

Vilamoura is an enormous and ambitious undertaking. As **Europe's biggest privately developed tourist complex** it covers an area of 1600 sea-side hectares only 20 kms away from Faro International Airport. **Lusotur**, the Portuguese company who owns Vilamoura and is responsible for its tremendous progress in the last few years, divided this huge area into several sectors. 600 hectares is for farming, 520 for property developments, hotels and holiday villages and 480 for parks, gardens, swimming pools and open spaces. This means that Vilamoura has one of the lowest occupation densities in Europe, as well as some of the best amenities. Two 18 hole par 73 golf courses designed by Frank Pennink, draw players from all over the world. The third (27 hole) course, designed by Joseph Lee has just opened. (See page 25). The world class Marina, now capable of receiving 1000 pleasure crafts and presently constructing a second phase with another 800 berths, will be the largest in southern Europe. Add to that a casino, riding, shooting, tennis, fishing and scuba diving, restaurants, shops and some spectacular **new hotels and property developments**, and you'll understand why Vilamoura is becoming so well known in Europe.

The marina acts as the social centre of this huge area. Near the marina too is the **Sales Office of Lusotur**, who will give you information about the area and help you find your way around.

For further information contact:
Lusotur Sales Office, Vilamoura, 8125 • Quarteira. Tel: 380088. Fax: 315934.

Bovis abroad *(at Quinta do Lago)*

Lakeside Village

Bovis Abroad, part of the **P&O Group**, now has three superb developments in the Algarve.

AT QUINTA DO LAGO:

2000 acres of pines, green fairways and lakes are the setting for Bovis Abroad's first two estates:

Lakeside Village is an established mix of Algarvian-style detached villas with private pools, plus one or two bedroom apartments grouped around the main pool.

Set in beautiful landscaping with water features, they nestle by the main lake with windsurfing and sailing, right by the Ria Formosa.

São Lourenço's luxury apartments form a crescent on a secluded wooden plateau, with views either of the lake or the exclusive 18-hole golf course.

Throughout the one to three bedroom apartments, the highest standards of building, interior design and finish are evident. Owners have membership rights to the Golf Club with its own restaurant and bar.

Bovis abroad *(at Lagos)*

Quinta da Boavista

In the Western Algarve - Quinta da Boavista is the natural development for Bovis Abroad's team that successfully established Lakeside Village and São Lourenço. In an area full of historical and cultural interest just over an hour from Faro International Airport and 2,5 km outside Lagos, the lovely 195-acre estate nurtures almond trees and wild flowers.

Realistically-priced three and four bedroom detached villas, each designed for its own individual plot, are arranged around courtyards and pools for maximum privacy.

The farmhouse style is mainly single-storey with traditional finishes and wrought ironwork. A restaurant, health club, hotel and village houses will complete the estate, a perfect base for exploring the Western Algarve.

Bovis Abroad's design options offer great choice to purchasers, plus planning permission for each plot, in this unique area of the Algarve with Government approved plans which safeguard the rural environment and beautiful rugged coastline with its secluded sandy bays.

For more information, contact: Bovis Abroad Limited, Quinta do Lago, Apartado 468, 8136 Almansil Codex, Algarve, Portugal. Tel: (089) 394794/ 396179, Fax: (089) 396155 or at Quinta da Boavista SA Sales Office: Tel: (082) 769685/7/8 Fax: (082) 769686.

P&O

Boa Vista *(Tavira)*

The Eastern Algarve is the almost undiscovered part of Portugal's Atlantic Coast. Its beaches stretch from the ancient town of Tavira to the Spanish border, and development is strictly controlled. Boa Vista is one of the few developments which have been permitted. It is a few kilometres from Tavira on an elevated site which slopes down to a small river. Here Goulden & Sons (Portugal) Ltd, a well established British property company, is building 80 exclusive villas on large, spacious plots. They offer a range of designs - or a design and build service. Above all, you can compare the value of what is available here with other parts of Portugal.

For example plot sizes are a minimum of about 2,500 sq metres, and build quality and materials are of the highest standard.

All this combined with easy access from either Faro (40 minutes to the West) or Spain (40 minutes to the East) makes Boa Vista one of the best investments on the Algarve.

Colour brochure and details from Castelo Estate Agents, Av. Dr. Mateus Teixeira de Azevedo, 44, 8800 Tavira. Tel: (081) 22774.

Algarve — region by region

FARO (7kms from Faro Airport)

Since the middle of the 18th century, Faro has been the capital of the Algarve. Though it has a long history - a bishopric in the 4th century and certainly a settlement on the site for well over 2.000 years - almost all its buildings were destroyed in an earthquake in 1755 and most of its finest buildings are comparatively modern. It was liberated from the Moorish domination in 1249 and a bronze statue in the main square honours King Afonso III who led the conquering Christian forces. Like so many other cathedrals in this region of Portugal and southern Spain, that at Faro was converted from a mosque. The old quarter of the town is still surrounded by parts of the ancient defensive walls and is worth visiting, since it is quite spectacular. See map on page 60 'Cidade Velha' section E.

Faro is also the first point of entry for foreign visitors to the Algarve arriving by plane, especially since the existing airport was renovated and expanded in 1989.

The airport is now capable of handling thousands more visitors every year.

Sightseeing. There are historic buildings worth seeing: **The Cathedral, the Nuns' Convent,** inside **the Town Hall, the Municipal Museum, the Ethnographic and Maritime Museum, the Church of Our Lady of Carmo.** A noted chapel of **Bones** and **Museum of Sacred Art:** the blue and white tiled **Church of St. Francis** and the old town gate **'Arco de Repouso'**.

Accommodation

HOTEL EVA (****) Overlooking the small harbour, the Hotel Eva has a rooftop restaurant with commanding view of the sea, and a terrace swimming pool, with bar service. 138 rooms, 12 suites with radio, telephone and private bath. Tel: (089) 803354, Telex: 56524.

HOTEL FARO (***) 44 rooms and 8 suites, all with private bath. The amenities include a special rooftop sundeck, a spacious barlounge, verandah-bar overlooking the yacht harbour and central city square. Very comfortable accommodation and a friendly atmosphere, very good value. Located in the city centre. Tel:803276. Cable Farotel-Faro. Special note: The front rooms have an excellent view. Telex: 5 61 08. Fax: 803546 P71, F3.

ESTALAGEM AEROMAR (****) 18 rooms with private bath. Located on Faro beach.Tel.817542

HOTEL ALBACOR (**) 38 double or twin bedrooms. All have private bathrooms. Bar lounge but not dining room. Rua Brites de Almeida, 23. Tel: 803593. P71. G1

CASA DE LUMENA (***) A picturesque Mansion with 12 bedrooms with bathrooms. Pleasant restaurant and Bar. In summer, there is the lovely "Grape Vine" Bar for snacks and drinks. All within minutes from Shopping Centre, Praca Alexandre Herculano, 27. Tel: 801990/1/2. Fax: 804019 P71, G10

PENSÃO 'O FARAÓ' (***) 28 rooms all with private bath. Restaurant. In city - Largo da Madalena, 4. Tel: 823356/824296/804997. P70, F5

SOLAR DO ALTO Sr. Guerreiro runs a very successful small hotel. All rooms have colour television, bathroom, telephone and heating. Bar and cafeteria, Rua do Berlim 55. Tel. 812869/812875.

LADY SUSAN. Newly renovated the LADY SUSAN offers an excellent choice of traditional and regional dishes. Seafood and shellfish are specialities. Relaxed air-conditioned atmosphere: Open for lunch 12.30 - 15.00 dinner 18.30 - 10.30. Closed Sundays. Rua 1.º de Dezembro, 28 (perpendicular to Rua Sto. António) Tel: 28857.

CIDADE VELHA. At long last the old walled city of Faro has an elegant restaurant set in its midst. The owner, Senhor Dias, a professional caterer makes certain that the international cuisine is of a high standard. Open for lunch, Mon-Fri 12.30-14.00. Dinner, Mon-Sat 19.30-22.30. Closed Sundays. Rua Domingos Guieiro Largo da Sé. Tel: 27145. P70. E27

Shopping. Faro's great attraction to the shopper is Rua Santo António - the pedestrianised High Street .

MAIN STREET, Two shops which have a very wide selection of local handicrafts, souvenirs and other quality items for the home or gifts. Well displayed. Rua Sto. António, 10, 21 and 29. P71G40.

ARESTA VIVA. A small atelier producing beautiful handmade and hanpainted wall tiles using authentic 16th century methods and colours. They have a permanent contract with the National Tile Museum in Lisbon to recreate 16th century wall friezes. They will undertake any design you wish, or buy the tiles ready-made. Contact them at; **Rua Antero de Quental 22, Faro. Tel. (089) 802187.**

SUPERMARKET SUPERGARBE operated by Portuguese with international experience. A wide selection of groceries and drinks - local and imported. Also many other items of daily necessity. Located across the Largo do Carmo from the Post Office. P70, B22.

Transportation facilities

AUTO UNIVERSO—a local company with years of experience. Main Office: Rua de S. Gonçalo de Lagos, 15, 8000 FARO, Tel: 22862/24833, Telex: 56341, Telefax: 20423.**Branches: Aeroporto de Faro** - Tel 27010/27905**Four Seasons - Quinta do Lago** - Tel. 96150/96172. **Information Center - Quinta do Lago** - Tel. 96768, **Vilamoura Marinotel - Vilamoura** - Tel. 33332/33310. P70, B11

AVIS, International car rentals. Faro Airport. Tel: 818538. Telex: 56737 P70 C12.

EUROPCAR INTERNACIONAL, ALUGUER DE AUTOMÓVEIS, LDA. Faro, Edifício Europcar, Estrada Aeroporto. Montenegro. Reservations Tel:818777. Telex: 56141 P. Faro Airport. Tel:818316 Fax: 818393. P70 B14.

AUTOCERRO - Vale das Almas
Estrada do Montenegro. 8000 FARO. Telefone: (089) 818427, 817670, 818434.

KENNING - Faro - (Airport) - Arrival Hall - 8000 Faro Tel: (089) 818351. Telex: 56781 Kentar P. Fax: (089) 818503 Faro - (Estrada do Aeroporto) Gambelas 8000 Faro Telefs: (089) 818145/6 - Telex: 56781 Kentar P. Fax: (089) 818503.

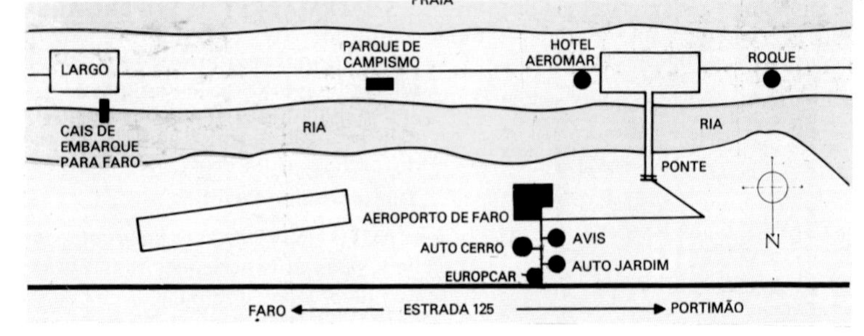

AGÊNCIA ABREU is the largest and oldest Portuguese Travel Organization, founded in Oporto in 1840. **ABREU** network includes 20 offices in Portugal, 15 in Brazil, Great Britain, Spain and U.S.A.. As the leading agent in Portugal we have experienced incoming departments for Tour Operators, Incentives, Special Groups, Congresses, Seminars, Meetings and Cargo. Hotels/Villas/Apartments/Self-DriveCars/Air/Rail/Sea/CoachTickets and Transfers for Groups and individuals are offered to our clients. **ABREU** operates official tours regularly. **Faro:** Av. da República, 124. Tel: 25035. Telex: 56720. Fax: 818144 **Portimão**: Rua Infante D. Henrique, 83 Tel: 416151. Telex: 57332 Fax: 416258. **Lisboa**: Av. da Liberdade, 160. Tel: 3476441 Telex: 12304 Fax: 3464614 **Porto:** Av. dos Aliados, 207. Tel: 324524 Telex: 22448. Fax: 200514 **Funchal:** Ed. Stª Catarina, Av. do Infante, 22 r/c - D Tel: 31077 Telex: 72234 Fax: 30952.

LINK INTERNATIONAL TRAVEL SERVICE. This handling agency has been established in the Algarve since 1979, with a young but well-experienced staff, experts in handling large charter operations, interest groups, sports groups, conventions and incentives. A welcome desk at the Faro Airport provides all the assistance. Rua Dr. Coelho de Carvalho, 1 , 8000 Faro. Tel: (089) 803483. Telex: 56744 Fax: (089) 28259 P71, C21.

STAR TRAVEL SERVICE — Rua Conselheiro Bivar, 36. Tel (089) 25125 Telex: 56768. P70 F63

MILTOURS — The leading specialists in incoming tourism to Portugal. Official land handling agents for top tour operators. Own fleet of modern motorcoaches offering extensive service in the Algarve, Lisbon and Oporto areas. Wide range of local excursions and coach tours. Full travel service. Hotel management. Jeep and safaris. Welcome desk at Faro Airport.

Head office: R. Veríssimo de Almeida, 14. Faro. Tel: 802030. Telex: 56336. Fax: 802037. **Branch Offices:** Praia da Rocha, Edifício Marivau — Loja 1. Tel: 416280. Telex: 56792 Fax: 416370. **Lisbon**: R. Conde Redondo, 21. Tel: 542268. Telex: 60428. Fax: 542988.

RN TOURS VIAGENS E TURISMO Appointed Agents IATA, ASTA, UFTAA, GRAY LINE, EUROPABUS and ICCA. Offices in Algarve (Faro, Albufeira, Portimão), Lisbon, Oporto, Évora, Santarém, Castelo Branco, Leiria and Coimbra. Welcome desks at Faro, Lisbon and Oporto airports. Hotel, Villa and Apartment arrangements, self drive cars, air/rail/sea/coach reservations and tickets, inclusive tours, coachhire and transfers for groups and individuals. Meetings and Convention organisers. Multilingual Guides. Also operates the official tours by coach in the Algarve, regularly and with guaranteed departures all year round. Please contact and ask for further details: **FARO**-Hotel EVA Building. Tel: 803305/6/7/8. Telex: 56525. **ALBUFEIRA**-Av. 25 de Abril. Tel 589030/1. Telex: 56201. **PORTIMÃO**-Rua Judice Biker. Tel: 25413-26178. Telex: 57381 P70, F55

TUROPA (incoming division Faro). This well-known agency specialises in handling incoming clients to the Algarve, and they will arrange special programmes according to the needs of each individual and group. Its founders and staff have many years of experience in the travel business, and all clients are handled with a high level of professional service and attention to detail. **Contact:** them at Rua Dr. José de Matos, 19, 8000 Faro. Tel: (089) 813611/813626/813688. Telex: 58364/58369. Fax: (089) 28245. TUROPA also has offices in Lisbon and Oporto.

Entertainment, Sitting in the garden by the yacht harbour in the centre of town on a summer evening and drinking coffee and local brandy with friends is a great pastime. It can also be a pleasant walk around the shops in the High Street and the back streets.

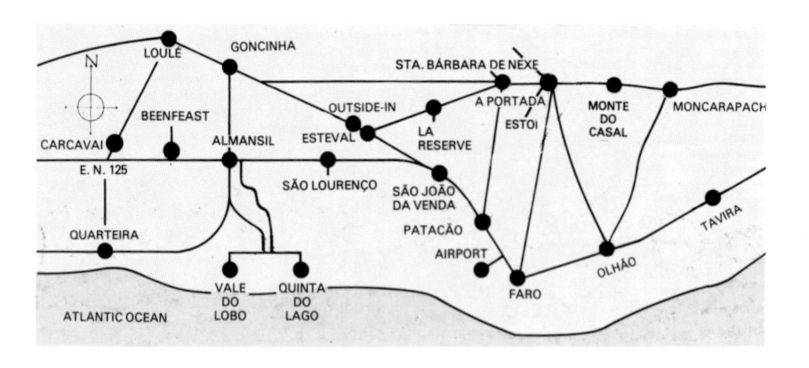

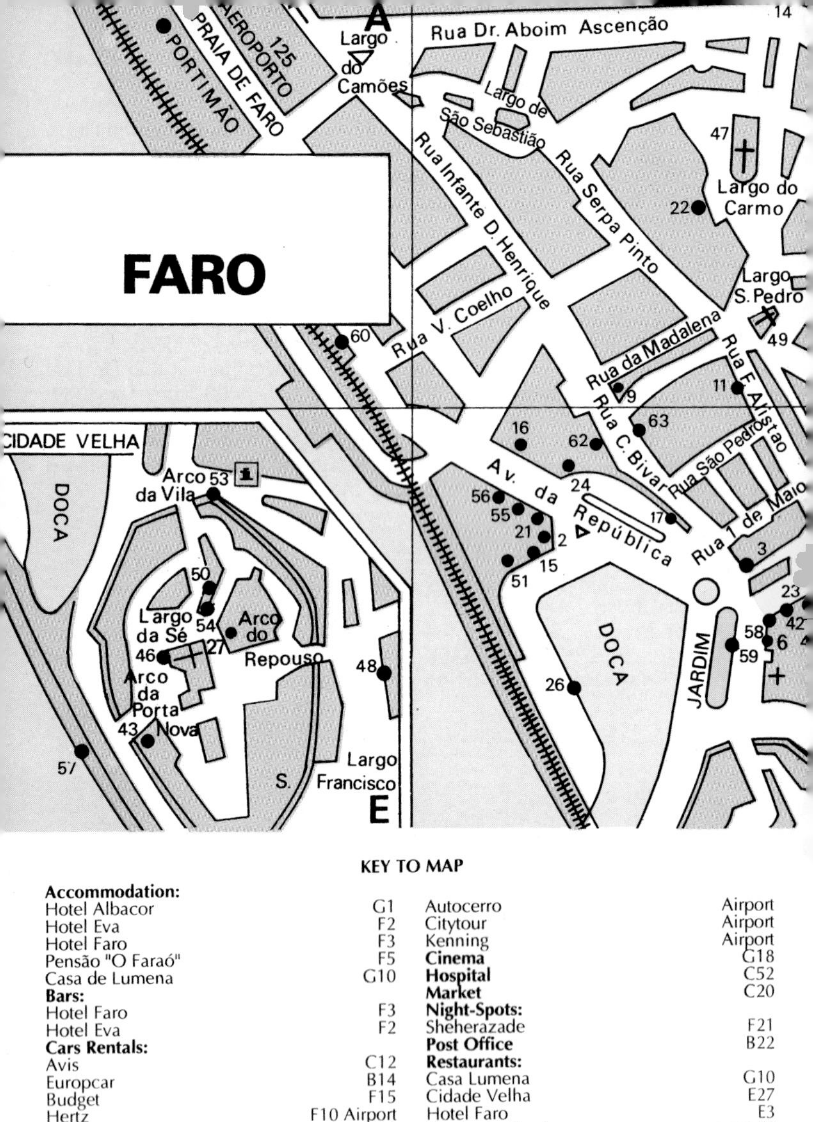

KEY TO MAP

Accommodation:	
Hotel Albacor	G1
Hotel Eva	F2
Hotel Faro	F3
Pensão "O Faraó"	F5
Casa de Lumena	G10
Bars:	
Hotel Faro	F3
Hotel Eva	F2
Cars Rentals:	
Avis	C12
Europcar	B14
Budget	F15
Hertz	F10 Airport
Auto Universo	B11
Autocerro	Airport
Citytour	Airport
Kenning	Airport
Cinema	G18
Hospital	C52
Market	C20
Night-Spots:	
Sheherazade	F21
Post Office	B22
Restaurants:	
Casa Lumena	G10
Cidade Velha	E27
Hotel Faro	E3
Monte do Casal	page 72

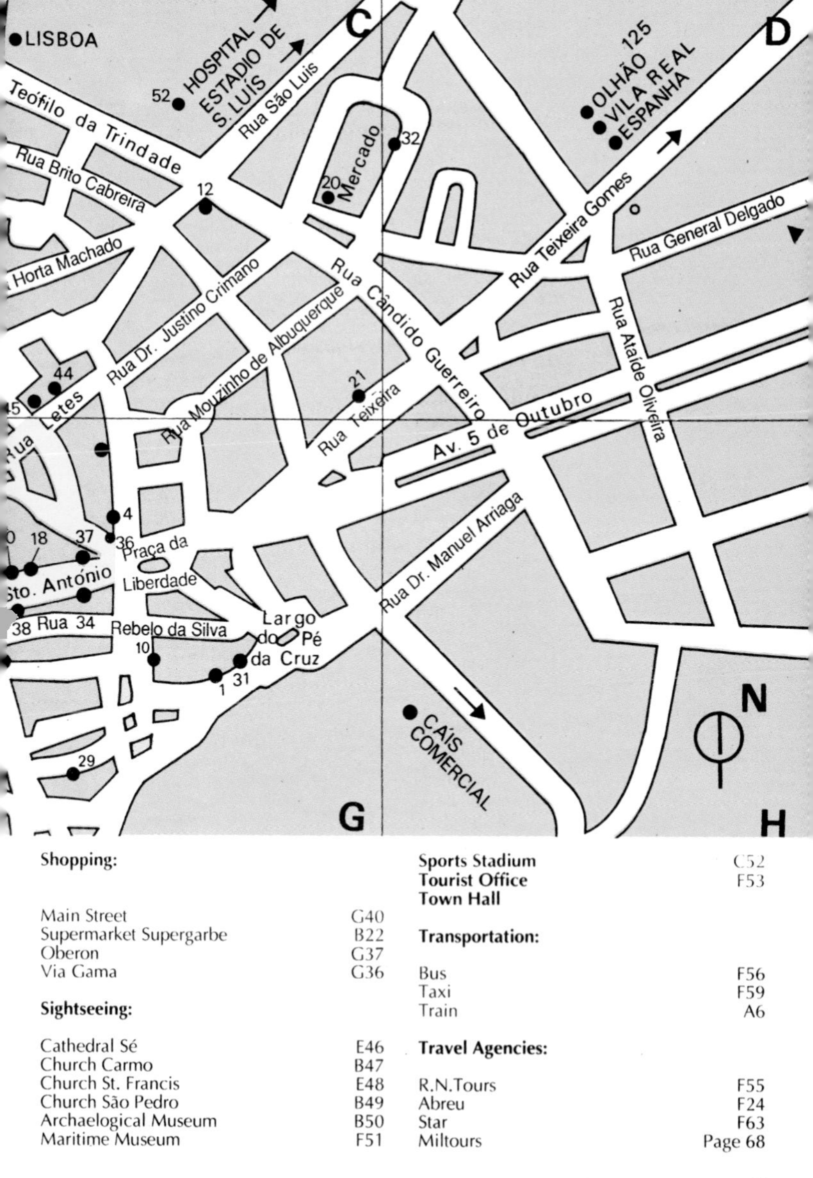

Shopping:

Main Street	G40
Supermarket Supergarbe	B22
Oberon	G37
Via Gama	G36

Sightseeing:

Cathedral Sé	E46
Church Carmo	B47
Church St. Francis	E48
Church São Pedro	B49
Archaeological Museum	B50
Maritime Museum	F51

Sports Stadium	C52
Tourist Office	F53
Town Hall	

Transportation:

Bus	F56
Taxi	F59
Train	A6

Travel Agencies:

R.N.Tours	F55
Abreu	F24
Star	F63
Miltours	Page 68

STA. BARBARA DE NEXE

(9 kms from Faro Airport)

INLAND ACCOMMODATION AND RESTAURANTS. As the beach areas become very busy more and more accommodation and restaurants are opening inland.

MONTE DO CASAL. Small and picturesque country inn set in the unspoilt Algarvean countryside with panoramic views to the sea. The attractive restaurant offers an excellent cuisine including gourmet-house specialities. Dining either in the old coach house or on the terrace, under the palm trees over-looking the floodlit pool. Carol and Bill Hawkins are your hosts and you can be assured of a very personal and warm welcome. Bill trained at the Savoy and Claridge's, London. They offer value for money and as the restaurant is not large, reservations are recomended. Tel: (089) 91503/91341. Telex: 56682 MONTCA P. Open for lunch and dinner. Closed Monday. For directions **follow the yellow signs from the church in Estoi.**

LA RESERVE. One of the best international cuisines with a strong French accent, a gourmet obligation. Reservations recommended. Near St. Bárbara de Nexe. Tel. (089) 90234. Closed Tuesdays.

LOULÉ

(15 kms from Faro Airport)

Though it is a large market town and has a number of interesting buildings, Loulé is best known as a **centre for craft workmanship.** In the main the craftsmen are the descendants of the Moslem community which gathered around Loulé at the time of the Christian conquest.

Sightseeing

Monuments. Castle walls from the Middle Ages. **Parish Church** in Gothic style from the 12 th century. The interior is worth a visit. Tiles from the 17th century, wood carvings and an unusual pulpit in wrought iron. Remarkable are the side altars of St. Michael and St. Bras. The latter has a fine wood sculpture of St. Brás from the early 16th century. **Church of Misericórdia.** Pórtico in Manueline style. In the churchyard there is a fine stone cross sculptured on both sides with the figure of Christ and Our Lady. **Ruined Monastery of Graça**; Gothic style from the 13th and 14th centuries is of great interest.

The Museum. Lies within the walls of an Arabic Castle captured from the Moors by the Portuguese in 1249. There are many works of art that have been discovered and collected over the years that form the basis of a fascinating collection. There are walks around the castle walls and towers which afford a magnificent view for miles around.

Car Hire

KENNING - Loulé - Turalgarve -Pç. Républica, 98/100 - Tel. 6 21 43.

Restaurants - Bars

O AVENIDA. A haven for visitors and shoppers to Loulé. A very pleasant atmosphere, and its open for lunch and dinner, except Sunday. Located near the roundabout in the centre of Loulé. Manuel Augusto is the friendly owner. **Tel: (089) 62106. Avenida José da Costa Mealha, 13, r/c.**

MARIA'S. Tino Correia's restaurant is becoming extremely well known for its excellent soups, freshly grilled fish and steaks with fine sauces. Or order one day before and try the house speciality, duck with orange. **On the road between Almansil and Loulé.** Tel: (089) 397164.

AUX BONS ENFANTS A small provincial-style French restaurant run by **Daphne and Didier.** Daphne learned cooking from her mother and grandmother, and then worked in St. Tropez. **Dinner only. Closed Sun.** 116 Rua Eng. Duarte Pacheco. Tel: (089) 62096.

O CARCAVAI.

Ingrid and Roger have brought a touch of best Belgian/French cooking to the Algarve. The country setting is complemented by an intimate atmosphere; there is a flower-filled patio for summer meals and lounge with log fire for colder days. Very good value for money. Located on the main Quarteira-Loulé road, 2.500 m after traffic lights (to Loulé on the left). Open dinner only 7.30 to 12.00. Closed Sats and December. Tel. 413565.

QUINTA DAS TÍLIAS On the road from Loulé to Alte, about 1 km from the outskirts of the town, the youthful Fernando Dias, trained in hotel management, runs a terrific bar in what seems at first a private house. A large pool table, open fire and the best Irish coffee have made it an instant success. Open 7.30 pm to late. Closed Mondays. Tel: (089) 415719.

ALMANSIL - QUINTA DO LAGO (20 kms approximately from Faro Airport)

QUINTA DO LAGO, is a spectacularly unspoilt estate of 1700 acres of pine forests, rolling grass, fresh water lakes and tidal inlets, a UNESCO - recognised wildlife sanctuary for rare species of birds migrating south. Some large plots are for sale and prospective owners are introduced to the finest local architects and builders to ensure each villa is truly original. The magnificent 36 hole golf course and the lake with its watersports are nearby. And owners automatically become members of **Club da Quinta**, which provides villa, garden and pool maintenance, rental services, maid, nanny and secretarial assistance, and a 24 hour security service. Or you can buy residential membership timeshare for yourself or your company at the **Quinta do Lago Country Club.** which is on the edge of the River Formosa, near the sea. And within the estate itself you have Shepherds restaurant, Patio nightclub, Gigi's beach bar and the Pergola on the Lagoon, and the Buganvilia shopping centre.

Contact Quinta do Lago, Almansil, 8100 Loulé, Algarve. Tel: (089) 394271/3 Telex: 56893 PLANAL P.

INTERNATIONAL HEALTH CENTRE Buganvilia Plaza. Here Dr. Woolfson is available for consultation.

April-Sept.	9.30	6.30	Mon-Fri
	10-1		Sat.
Oct-March	10-1	3-6	Mon-Fri

Tel: (089) 396157/396169.

Doctor available 24 hours a day 7 days a week — emergency number (089) 396157.

HOTEL QUINTA DO LAGO (*****) Half an hour's drive from Faro airport, in the midst of 1860 acres of pine woods and rolling hills, and overlooking a beautiful beach and tidal inlet full of protected species of rare birds, lies the Hotel Quinta do Lago. It possesses 141 luxury rooms and 9 suites. All rooms have airconditioning, balconies and satellite television. The Hotel also boasts its own tennis courts (with resident pro), billiards room, heated indoor and outdoor pools, an extensive Health Club with massage facilities and a gymnasium, and even function rooms for larger gatherings. The hotel has a speciality restaurant, named the Ca d'Oro which serves expertly prepared Italian cuisine. Then there is the Navegadores Restaurant which offers a varied menu that includes many traditional Portuguese dishes. Light meals are also served beside the pool. The bar overlooking the beach is well worth a visit. Outside the hotel itself but within the estate there are superb sporting facilities. The Quinta do Lago golf courses are among the top ten in Europe. They offer 4 nine hole courses, and are designed by William Mitchell. The Algarve's other courses are all within a short drive of the hotel. Riding stables are nearby. Windsurfing and watersports are practiced on the estate's 29 acre inland saltwater lagoon. The hotel is managed by the Orient Express Hotels chain and is a member of the Leading Hotels of the World. **Hotel Quinta do Lago, 8135 Almancil, Tel: (089) 396666, Fax: (089) 396393, Telex: 57118 HOQDLP.**

HOTEL DONA FILIPA (*****) The exclusive Vale de Lobo estate surrounds the Hotel Dona Filipa. For sports enthusiasts or beach loving holiday makers this is an idyllic spot. Guests of the hotel can play golf free on the newly-aquired 18 hole golf course at nearby **San Lorenzo**, free green fees are also available at the Dona Filipa's sister hotel the Penina Golf, near Portimão, which boasts another superb course of its own.

All rooms are air conditioned, with private bathrooms and sun terraces. Good food and wine are an important hallmark of the Dona Filipa, and the restaurant and **Terrace Grill** offer splendid international cuisine. There is also a poolside bar/restaurant.

The hotel also has three all weather tennis courts, with the **Roger Taylor Tennis School** only minutes away. The less ambitious can enjoy the hotel's large swimming pool, or wander along the sandy beach.

Contact Dona Filipa Hotel, Vale de Lobo, 8136 Almansil, Algarve. Tel (089) 394141 telex 56848 Fax 394288. TRUSTHOUSE FORTE HOTELS.

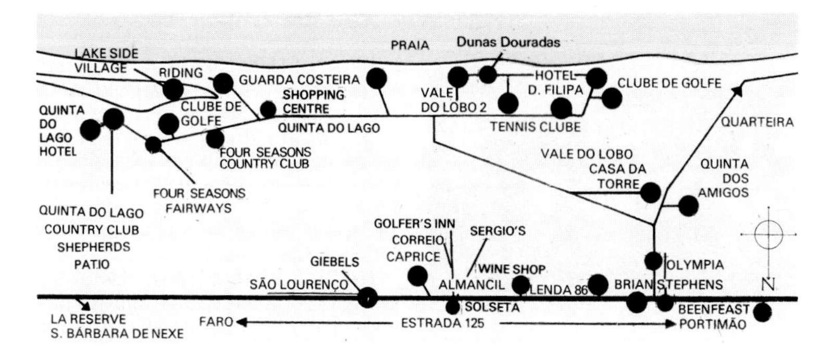

Restaurants - Bars - Nightspots

CAPRICE . Don't let the roadside appearance put you off, just move around to the back for parking and then step into an attractive Portuguese ambience. The menu is international and of very good quality. Closed Saturdays.Tel: 395848.

O TRADICIONAL - This 1884 Algarvian farmhouse has been restored to house a brasserie-style restaurant whose menu changes daily according to the local produce available. The French chef produces authentic cooking in a relaxed, informal atmosphere. The maitre d' is the charming Sr. Joaquim, who will guide you through the menu. On the Almancil-Quarteira road before the Vale de Lobo turnoff. Open for dinner only. Tel. (089) 399093.

SHEPHERD'S RESTAURANT AND PATIO NIGHTCLUB. Right next door to Quinta do Lago Country Club is Shepherd's, one of the Algarve's most famous restaurants, run by Richard Shepherd of the renowned Langan's Brasserie in London. At the elegant Patio Club next door you can talk, relax, drink and dance into the small hours. Tel: (089) 394541 .

GOLFER'S INN. Almansil now has its own pub restaurant - and in grand style and at great expense. Five cosy dining areas tastefully decorated with old bits of the past. Outside grill area and a separate bar/dining area for golfers and special events. Bending the elbow and dining here with friends can be fun and pleasant. Rua 5 de Outubro. Tel: 395725.

BRASSERIE DES AMIS. Catherine, the owner, has created a very pleasant wine bar/bistro in the heart of Almansil. Freshly cooked dishes appear on the menu every day. Marvellous homemade puddings. Italian, French and German wines by the glass. Rua do Comércio. Tel: 399313.

INDIA Tandoori Restaurant. Chandra Patel, the ower, serves authentic Indian food in this elegantly-appointed restaurant. The family is from Gujarati in Northwest India and tandoori chicken, traditional curries, vegetarian entreés, and tandoori bread are just some of the specialities. The decor is austere but soothing. Open for dinner every night except Sunday. Tel. (089) 395756.

ALMANSIL

Restaurants

OLYMPIA. Long established and well known for their fresh charcoal grilled fish and meat dishes. Located Quarteira - Vale do Lobo turn off on main road (then 125m on right-hand side). Closed Monday. Tel: 395397.

SERGIO'S - The restaurant 'Brown Jug' is now more spacious. Outside garden terrace. Varied, good cuisine. Friendly and relaxing atmosphere. In front of Post Office, Tel: 395154.

TINO'S - Vale do Lobo (near the super-market). International cooking with French specialities, flambées, shellfish by order. Terrace in the summer. Reservations recommended, Private parking. Tel: 394656. (Closed Sunday).

SÃO GABRIEL - Excellent five star food and service in this newly opened restaurant. It is subdued, quiet, elegant and serves international cuisine. On the road between Quinta do Lago and Vale de Lobo. Open for dinner only from 7 to 11pm. Closed Mondays. Tel: (089) 394521.

Real estate

BRIAN STEPHENS LDA. Brian and Pam along with son Mark are old hands on the Algarve. Specialists in property sales, construction, management and rental of luxury villas in Quinta do Lago, Vale do Lobo and Almansil areas **Office**: Rua 5 de Outubro, Almansil. Tel: (089) 395729/395320. Fax: (089) 395355. Telex: 56013.

GIEBELS REAL ESTATE Here is a property company (Dutch) that is small enough to offer reasonable prices and yet big enough to give a wide and efficient service in all aspects of property dealings, such as the care of the intricate legalities,making one's purchase trouble free. The Giebels have been here since 1970. Their office is on the main Faro-Portimão road (EN 125). The Government-licensed Real Estate Agency has hundreds of properties on its books, be it land, a villa, an old farmhouse, an apartment or a business. Their associated government-licensed Building Company can design and build anything from a farmhouse conversion to a 20 room mansion to superior quality pools, all at reasonable prices with a written guarantee. Extensive property lists and villa and pool brochures available. 'Peace of Mind is Part of the Deal' **GIEBELS Lda**, Estrada Nacional, 125, S. Lourenço, 8135 Almansil. Tel: (089) 395353 GIEBEL P Fax: (089) 397098.

Travel

SOLSETA TRAVEL AGENCY. IATA agents in Almansil. Specialists in renting Villas with/without pool, self drive car hire air/sea/coach/rail and hotels/apartments reservations. Rua Duarte Pacheco, 174, Almansil, 8135 Almansil, Algarve. Tel: (089) 395278/ 395298. Telex: 56078 SOLSET P.

Introduction

The Vilamoura area, made up of the former fishing village of Quarteira and the 3,800 acres of land surrounding the marina at Vilamoura, is a fine example of the controlled creation of nothing less than a large town, with tourism as its livelihood.

The whole area benefits from a wide sandy beach, which formerly provided Quarteira with its fishing. Now Quarteira is transformed into a bustling town with discos, nightlife, and restaurants.

Vilamoura itself, however, is a world apart. Created 25 years ago by the far-sighted Artur Cupertino de Miranda, this huge estate now offers every facility for residents and visitors alike. Strictly controlled in planning terms, the area around the Marina boasts luxury hotels and apartments, while further away there are several prestigious property developments. Within Vilamoura there is an airstrip, three golf courses, a shooting range, big game fishing, tennis clubs, yacht hire, one of the largest horseriding centres in Europe, a large sports complex, casinos, scuba diving and all manner of other sports, shops and leisure activities. And don't forget the largest marina in southern Europe!

Real Estate

VENDAVILLA — VILAGENT: This very well regarded estate agency specialises in resales and new projects in Vilamoura. Well established, with experienced lawyers to handle property purchases. See them at Edifício do Cinema, Loja 3, Vilamoura. (Opposite the Casino). Tel: (089) 314486. Fax: (089) 315.

QUARTEIRA (24 kms from Faro Airport)

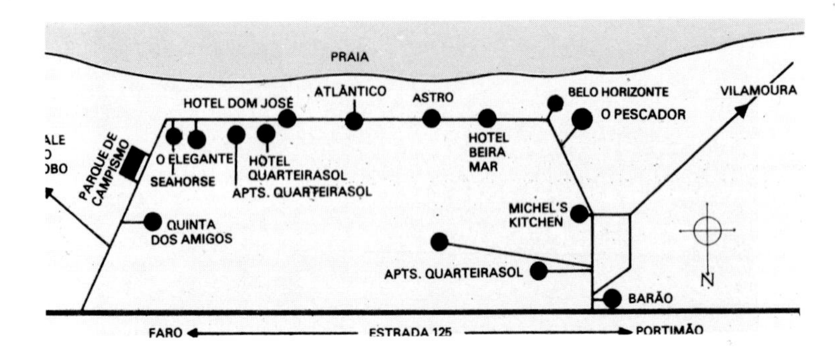

Accommodation

HOTEL DOM JOSÉ (* * *) 146 rooms, all with private bath. Located on the beach. Reservations: Tel 314350. Cable Toca-Quarteira. Swimming pool and dancing. Telex: 56823.

Restaurants - Bars

ADEGA DO PEIXE. Famous among the locals for their grilled fresh fish and seafood. The airy black and white beamed restaurant has a bar downstairs and food upstairs, with a great view over the beach. Open for lunch and dinner. Av. Infante Sagres. Tel: 312686.

ROSA BRANCA. Sr. Teixeira runs this large restaurant looking over Quarteira's long sandy beach. With an outdoor terrace, it's ideal for a drink, snack, or dinner or lunch. Fresh fish and aquariums filled with live seafood mean you can pick the one you want! Av. Infante Sagres, Tel: 314430.

O PESCADOR. Portuguese operated. Don't let the plain decor or size put you off. Has a well established reputation for fresh fish and Portuguese dishes. The fish market is across the road. Tel: 314755.

Shopping

ASTRO - A Wonderful Shop! The centre point in Quarteira for a wide variety of newspapers, magazines, tobacco, perfumery, handicrafts. Located on main Avenida Infante de Sagres 41 . Tel: 312126,

Transportation facilities

AVIS. Centro Comercial Abertura Mar. Tel: 314519. Telex: 56737 P.

BUDGET-RENT-A-CAR, Av. Infante Sagres. Tel: 313046/313837.

TOP TOURS, a leading Travel Agency and Tour Operator with a nationwide network. **Algarve** office situated at Av. Infante de Sagres, 73-8125 Quarteira Tel: (089) 312726/ 313972. Branch offices also in **Oporto** and **Funchal**, Head office in **Lisbon**: Rua Luciano Cordeiro, 116 - 1000 Lisboa. Tel: (01) 560913/560923.

Accommodation

The **DOM PEDRO HOTEL GROUP** is one of the best known in Portugal and has three superb hotels in Vilamoura, benefiting from the estate's sporting facilities; **HOTEL DOM PEDRO GOLF (****)** has 261 rooms, all facing the sea, with balcony, telephone, radio, satellite TV and air conditioning. There are 2 heated pools and 1 for children, 3 floodlit courts, a nearby beach, bars, restaurants and conference facilities. Tel: (089) 889650. Fax; 315482. Telex: 56149 PEDROV P.

SUITEHOTEL D. PEDRO PORTOBELO (****) has 138 suites with balcony, complete with telephone, radio, satellite TV, and air conditioning, kitchenette, full bathroom and sea views from all the suites. There is a restaurant, bar and supermarket, and 2 pools. All Vilamoura's facilities are nearby. Tel: (089) 889603. Telex: 58339.

HOTEL DOM PEDRO MARINA (****) has 154 rooms with telephone, radio, satellite TV, mini bar, and airconditioning, and fabulous suites with private jacuzzi; and marvellous views. There is the DaPietro restaurant and bar and all the sporting facilities of the nearby sister hotels and Vilamoura itself .The hotel has a heated pool with jet stream.Tel: (089) 889802. Fax: 313270. Telex: 56307.

VILAMOURA (25 kms from Faro airport)

Accommodation

ALDEIA DO MAR. An attractive village of apartments and villas — 1,000-bed capacity. The many amenities include restaurants, snack bar, swimming pool, 2 tennis courts, mini golf and diving school, sports ground and the use of Vilamoura's sports facilities. Tel: 315135/315155/315105/314038. Telex: 56839 ADEMAR, Fax: (089) 315195.

VILAMOURA MARINOTEL (*****) Algarve's most luxurious hotel, overlooking the beach, sea and Vilamoura Marina. 388 bedrooms — all of them equipped with colour TV, video, radio, directdial telephone, minibar. For information: Tel: (089) 389988 Fax: 389869 Telex: 58827 MAROTE P.

HOTEL ATLANTIS VILAMOURA (*****) 305 rooms. The 14-storey hotel occupies a prime site overlooking the magnificent Vilamoura yacht basin. Bars, smart lounges, an indoor and outdoor swimming pool, a health centre and banqueting and conference facilities. Tel: 312535 / 312636 / 312575 / 312595. Telex: 56838.

PRADO VILLAS. These spacious and well-equipped villas can accommodate up to six people and are ideally situated in a quiet part of the pinewoods of the Vilamoura Estate. They are convenient both for all three of Vilamoura's golf courses, and the beach, which is a short drive away. Inclusive holidays are operated from the UK by The Travel Club of Upminster. For further details contact them direct at Station Road, Upminster, Essex, RM14 2TT. Phone: Upminster (04022) 25000. Telex 897124. Fax: (04022) 29678.

GOLF COUNTRY CLUB VILAMOURA (***). Now part of the famous Salvor Hotel group, this motel offers 52 rooms and suites, with private terraces, around its private pools. Here you benefit from all Vilamoura's amenities, splendid golf courses, the Casino, tennis, shooting and all other sports imaginable. It has a pitch and putt course, unique in the Algarve. Golf 1 is 100m, Golf 2 400m, and Golf 3 2kms. Truly a golfer's paradise! **Tel: (089) 302975, Fax: 302976.**

Restaurants

A MARGARIDA. At long last the Vilamoura Marina has an excellent restaurant owned and operated by professionals of long-standing. International cuisine. Interior decor soft and comfortable. Lovely setting, overlooking Marina. Tel: 312168.

Restaurants/Bars

A CASA DO LARGO/ALIGATOR'S Old Village, Vilamoura Tel. 380103
Three minutes from the Marina, in the picturesque heart of this traditional village, Vicky Martins has created a lively restaurant and bar. It is traditional Portuguese cooking - duck, fresh fish soup, chicken and fish "bouillabaise", and mouth watering sweets. After a delightful meal you can dance and enjoy the music from the 50's and 60's downstairs, at the Aligator's, with a fantastic band playing till 2.00.

PRINCESS GARDEN Located in the heart of the beautiful Old Village, overlooking pools and gardens, the restaurant offers the finest of traditional Peking cuisine. Expert Chinese chefs blend the freshest ingredients and oriental spices and present beautiful dishes. Follow signs to the Old Village. Tel: (089) 389726/380102.

Sport

CEPEMAR LDA, ALGARVE'S BIG GAME FISHING CENTER operates three highly sophisticated fishing boats, one from Vilamoura. Book through CEPEMAR, Lda. Praça da República, 24A, 8500 Portimão. **Tel (082)25866** Telex: 57348, and at Vilamoura Marina Pier Q-5 **Tel: (089) 312836. Mini Cruises are also available upon request.**

Transportation facilities

AVIS. Hotel Dom Pedro, Tel: 314519.

EUROPCAR INTERNACIONAL Aluguer de Automóveis, Lda.
Delta Marina Loja 1. Tel: 314883. Fax: 314883.

AUTO UNIVERSO — Vilamoura Marinotel. Tel: 313332/313310.

Travel

Algarve Marina Tours
Apart from being a full service travel agency that can handle all your travel needs, this company is also the experienced specialist in luxury guided motor-coach tours to all the major points of interest in the Algarve and beyond. Their high quality is maintained by their client questionnaire which takes place at the end of each tour.

Departures from Vale de Lobo/Quinta do Lago/Quarteira/Vilamoura/ Albufeira/Armação de Pêra
1) Boat Trip Tuesdays
2) Algarve Evening Tuesdays
3) Lisbon and Central Portugal Tuesdays (3 day tour)
4) Eastern Algarve Wednesdays
5) Seville and Jerez de la Frontera Wednesdays (2 day tour)
6) Lisbon (1 day tour) Thursdays
7) Historic Algarve Fridays
8) The Old Algarve Saturdays
9) Bullfight Saturdays
10) Lisbon (2 day tour) Mondays

Departures from Carvoeiro/Praia de Rocha/ Alvor/Lagos
1) Lisbon/Central Portugal Tuesdays (3 day tour)
2) Eastern Algarve Wednesdays
3) Seville/Jerez de la Frontera Thursdays
4) Lisbon (1 day tour) Thursdays
5) Wonderful Algarve Saturdays
6) Lisbon/Estoril (2 day tour) Sundays

Departures from Monte Gordo/Altura/ Tavira
1) Lisbon/Estoril Sundays (2 day tour)
2) Lisbon/Central Portugal Tuesdays (3 day tour)
3) Seville/Jerez de la Frontera Wednesdays (2 day tour).

For reservations and more information please contact your travel agent, hotel porter, travel representative or their office at Centro Comercial de Marina. 8125 Vilamoura Tel. (089) 302772/3/4 Fax. (089) 302775 Telex 56846

FALÉSIA - PRAIA OLHOS DE ÁGUA -DA OURA

(29 kms approximately from Faro Airport)

HOTEL ALFAMAR (****) ALFA MAR VILLAS & APARTMENTS - a key Convention and Sports Centre situated on famous Falésia beach, 25 minutes from Faro Airport, not far from Albufeira. Excellent accommodation - hotel rooms with ocean views, villas, studios, apartments, total 1500 beds. Exhibition Centre and Convention rooms, 18 championship tennis courts, clay, allweather courts and covered tennis. Also 2 squash courts, horseriding facilities, bowling, kegeln, crazy golf, bicycles, surfing, boating and fishing trips. Recreation, fitness and Health Centre with covered pool, sauna, whirlpool. Running tracks and runways, playgrounds (105x70 meters). Hotel owed rent a car and buses. Public bus stop at the hotel. Only 15 minutes to the Casino, bullfigth, Marina and four golf courses.

Tel: (089) 501351/4. Telex: 56840 ALFMAR P. F ax: (089) 501404.

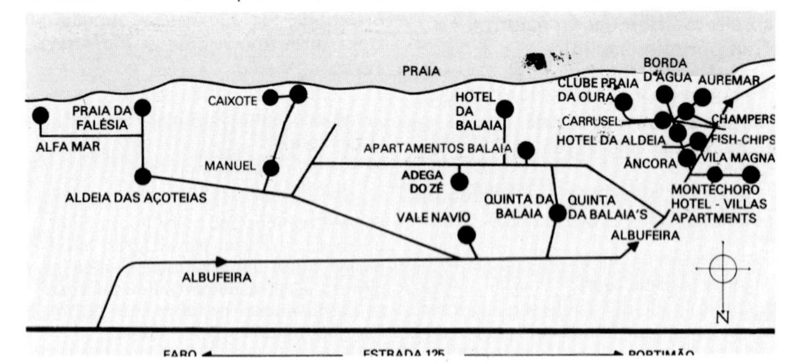

ALBUFEIRA (36 kms from Faro Airport)

The largest resort on the Algarve coast, Albufeira can claim to be the tourist capital of the region and has even been christened its St. Tropez. Though the main square is surrounded by souvenir shops and supermarkets, the atmosphere of the town is essentially Moorish, with hundreds of white houses straggling out from that centre and hugging the nearby hillsides. It has many cafes, restaurants, bars and discotheques. The town is right on the sea shore and its main beach is reached through a tunnel which leads from the main central shopping street, close by the Sol e Mar Hotel which dominates the beach. Its development has been rapid but a great deal of its character has been retained. Nowhere is this more evident than in the area around the fish market where there are many small restaurants. During the campaign to drive the Moors from southern Portugal, Albufeira was an important fortress town and was, in fact, one of the last to hold out against the Christian forces. It finally fell to King Afonso III in 1250. The most striking building is arguably the old town hall whose belfry tricks most visitors into thinking it is a church! Albufeira's own beach is quite good, though it tends to become crowded during the summer. Other excellent sandy beaches nearby are **São Rafael** to the west and **Olhos d'Água** to the east.

Sightseeing. Apart from the narrow, white painted streets with their Moorish arches which make walking pleasant in the town itself, there are walks along the cliff tops which present the visitor with excellent views.

Albufeira was the first town in the Algarve to be discovered by travellers in the 1960s and it continues to offer the widest choice in accommodation of any town in the Algarve. Visitors can either choose a reasonably priced "pensão" or hotel in the town itself, or venture outwards to the property resorts and hotels just outside the town centre. In the following pages we will indicate some of the best value and best quality accommodation, but worth a special mention is the 5 star Sheraton Hotel just outside Albufeira at Açoteias. This hotel will be possibly the most luxurious in the Algarve and has its own 9 hole golf course, for the exclusive use of hotel guests and residents of nearby luxury houses.

Until it opens contact (089) 395244/ 395255 for further details and bookings.

CLUB ALBUFEIRA

This Algarvian style village, consisting of one and two bedroomed apartments and cluster villas, lies in a sheltered valley one mile north of Albufeira. They are surrounded by beautifully landscaped gardens and have use of a large new swimming pool. Owners and clients also have use of the shops, bars, restaurants and sports facilities adjoining the village. Other amenities include an efficient reception and well-stocked supermarket and even a disco-club. Close to a variety of beaches and golf-courses.

Estrada de Ferreiras, 8200 Albufeira
Tel. (089) 587627 Fax. (089) 589393
Telex. 58571 ALCLUB F.

HOTEL MONTECHORO (****) is near the lovely fishing town of Albufeira in the centre of the Algarve coast. Montechoro takes pride in being the most modern and ambitious project in the area. The Hotel is impressive and spacious, enabling guests to enjoy the year-round warm, sunny and restful Algarve climate, in an atmosphere which will appeal to the most discriminating traveller.

The Hotel has 314 superb, spacious, air-conditioned rooms, and 48 fine suites. **The Montechoro Restaurant** is one of the highest gastronomic standard and the **Das Amendoeiras** rooftop Grill is in an elegant setting with an amazing panoramic view. Guests also have at their disposal 4 bars, one of which is the elegant **Almohade Piano-Bar** for relaxing before and after dinner; the **Bambu Bar** featuring live music and every Tuesday, a folklore show presented by local entertainers; lounge; congress rooms; swimming pools; 8 tennis courts; 2 squash courts; gymnasium; Health Club; hairdressing salon; shops and many other services to satisfy a discerning clientele. There are also conference facilities for up to 1500 delegates.

MONTECHORO HOLIDAY VILLAGE is part of the overall complex with villas and apartments, each fully equipped. The village has all the amenities of a resort area. Information: Montechoro, Apartado 928. Albufeira. Tel: 589423. Telex: 56288 P. Fax: 589947.

ALBUFEIRA - Accommodation

MONTECHORO BEACH CLUB - A prime development with a spectacular view of the open sea. Located just off one of Algarve's best beaches, Praia da Oura. The apartments are built and furnished to a very high standard in a total of 200 apartments. The whole holiday resort idea has been very well planned - 2 swimming pools, a health club, games room, reception/bar area and other amenities. Their Time-Share programme is very well defined. A part of the Montechoro Group. **For information:** Montechoro Beach Club, Apartado 761, Areias de S. João, 8200 Albufeira. Tel: 588486 Telefax: 589332 Telex: 58839 MBCLUB P.

HOTEL DA ALDEIA (****) — 2 kms from Albufeira, at Praia da Oura, the hotel has 128 rooms and 5 suites. Satelite TV, radio, telephone. Its traditional architecture includes large terraces, 2 swimming pools, tennis courts, mini golf, a bar, restaurant, Piano Bar with live music, games rooms and conference rooms for 120 people. The village also offers shops, hairdressers, a health club, gym, and squash. Golf courses and the Casino are nearby. Avenida Dr. Francisco Sá Carneiro, Areias de São João. Tel: (089) 588861. Fax: 588864. Telex: 56232.

HOTEL BOA VISTA (****) — 93 rooms and suites with satelite TV, radio, telephone and jacuzzi facing the sea. Near the action of the town centre, the hotel is still relaxing. There is a large swimming pool and sun terrace, coffee shop, lounge and tennis courts, and a famous restaurant overlooking the bay. Golf courses and the Casino are nearby. Rua Samora Barros, 6. Tel: (089) 589175/6/7. Fax. (089) 588836. Telex: 56204.

APARTHOTEL VILA MAGNA ALBUFEIRA JARDIM (****) 470 attractively furnished and fully equipped 1, 2 and 3-room apartments, all with full bath and telephone and balcony providing a beautiful view over town and sea. 5 swimming pools, one heated in winter with large sundeck. Also 3 tennis courts and first class restaurant PANORAMA, snackbars and bars, snooker and supermarket. Albufeira - Tel: 586972/6. Telex: 56258. Fax: 586977 P.93.C

APARTAMENTOS DA BALAIA (1st class). One of Algarve's most modern and best managed. 120 fully furnished apartments of very high standard with a direct telephone system. Excellent Lounge, Bar, Restaurant and Bar-Grill facilities. Also Gaming Room, two separate pools - (adults and childrens) and a Supermarket. Located 5 kms from Albufeira and close to the Maria Luisa beach (one of the finest). Tel: 50512/ 50519/52772. Telex: 56913 SOTUR P. Fax. 50314.

ESTALAGEM DO CERRO (****) 83 rooms all with private bath, colour TV, balconies overlooking the town and the beautiful bay. Swimming pool, (heated) gimnasium, health club, restaurant, bar, coffee shop. Tel: (089) 586191. Telex: 56211, Fax: 586194.

BEACH VILLAS OF CAMBRIDGE. Offering the best choice of UK flights and self-catering cottages and villas with private swimming pools. For information/brochure, contact: Beach Villas Limited, 8 Market Passage, Cambridge, CB2 3QR. Tel: (0223) 311113, or Albufeira Tel: 55816.

CERRO ALAGOA HOTEL (****) This aparthotel is situated on the edge of picturesque Albufeira overlooking the sea. The hotel boasts 310 rooms all equipped with minibar, direct dial telephone, satelite TV and radio. There are also several conference rooms. The hotel's unique feature is the indoor "jungle" swimming pool. There is also a poolside bar and an outdoor pool. The hotel health club has a jacuzzi and sauna. Downstairs there is an English Pub, and the Copacabana Restaurant, which offers food with a Brazilian and international flavour. Apartado 2155, 8200 Albufeira.
Tel: (089) 588261 Fax: (089) 588262
Telex 58290

Accommodation

THE TRAVEL CLUB OF UPMINSTER. Founded in the 1936, The Travel Club of Upminster is the largest tour operator to the Algarve offering four and five star hotels and self-catering apartments and villas, many with private swimming pools. Flights are on Sundays at convenient timings during the day to Faro from Gatwick, Heathrow, Standsted, Birmingham and Manchester throughout the year. For a copy of there brochure detailing holidays in the Algarve contact them direct at The Travel Club of Upminster, Station Road, Upminster, Essex, RM14 2TT. Phone: Upminster (04022) 25000. Telex 897124. Fax: (04022) 29678.

FAZENDA CARAVELA. These 20 villas, all architect designed, are situated on a small, secluded and very peaceful estate in the hills above Alcantarilha. Each villa can accommodate up to six people and each has its own private swimming pool. Inclusive holidays are operated from the UK by The Travel Club of Upminster. **For further details contact them direct at Station Road, Upminster, Essex, RM14 2TT. Phone: Upminster (04022) 25000. Telex 897124. Fax: (04022) 29678.**

Restaurants

O MONTINHO - Famous beautifully restored 18th century Portuguese farmhouse where French chef Joel Jouin serves delicate dishes from the freshest of local produce. Open for dinner only. **Located to the east of Albufeira behind Hotel Montechoro. Tel (089) 513959.**

A RUÍNA. Typically Portuguese. A long standing centre point for a wide variety of seafood supplied daily by local fishermen. The rustic multi-storey building starts with a beach snack bar, leads to a street level homely dining area with its adega and then on to the second floor's elegant dining room with its own kitchen. On the top floor is a bar and an open air snack area. Tel: 512094. Bar Terrace. Tel: (089) 589912. *P92, H34.*

'THE BEACH BASKET', Cabaz da Praia. Here it is pleasant to dine in the open air on the cliffside terrace with its beautiful sea view, complemented by an appetising international menu. Reservations recommended. Tel: (089) 512137. Located west of the Sol e Mar Hotel. *P92, G31.*

JARDIM d'ALLAH. Family operated specialising in Portuguese cuisine. Located in the ancient quarter of the city, the decor is Arabic and most attractive. Entrance is opposite the Hotel Sol e Mar. Tel: 52296. *P92, G22.*

West of Albufeira - Pera road, there are very good bars and restaurants.

ATLÂNTICO — Portuguese. Attractive courtyard, split level restaurant. Spacious and very good service with good food at reasonable prices. Well recommended. Closed Mondays. Rua General Humberto Delgado, 25-35. Tel: (082) 561678. GUIA.

PORTAS DO SOL. Restaurant-bar, a pool edge setting in São Rafael, the lovely countryside urbanization located off the Albufeira-Pera road. Professional staff and good food. Tel: (089) 52234.

East of Albufeira there is great activity. Areias S.º João, Montechoro.

BORDA D'AGUA, Located on the delightful Praia da Oura beach overlooking the sea is a complex of restaurants and bars. Here amidst this attractive setting there is always a wide selection of seafood supplied by local fishermen. On the first floor is the main restaurant-bar with its good Portuguese and international cuisine and Disco Bar. In the ground level restaurant, the specialities are grilled fish and meat. Tel: (089)586545.

CASA BITOQUE. This elegant restaurant is a must for visitors who enjoy homemade Italian food. It is an old town house tastefully restored by its owners. The food is outstanding - freshly made ravioli, carpaccio, lamb with ratatouille and herbs, pasta in seafood and white wine sauce, and best of all the desserts, among which there is the delicious white and dark chocolate terrine with yoghurt sauce. Situated in the little village of Guia. Open every evening 7 to 12. Closed Sunday **Rua do Poço 8200 Guia. Reserve on (089) 561665.**

The management of these three highly recommended restaurants have a success story going back over 19 years and, not without justification, they claim to "cater for every taste".

ÂNCORA — Old established restaurant, bar, and grill room renowned for good food, efficient service and friendly atmosphere. Grilled specialities are served on the "Top Deck" terrace. Easy to find at the Oura crossroads. Live and different musical entertainment provided every evening. Open from 9am to 2am each day for breakfast, lunch, dinner and snacks. Tel.: 512665. *P85.*

CARRUSEL — Restaurant, terrace grill and bar, at the top of the hill above Praia da Oura — is now a firm favourite with summer and winter holiday-makers alike, both for its reasonably priced good food and the very congenial atmosphere with varied music and entertainment nightly. The "Saucy Chicken" next door serves grilled dishes either inside or outside in the garden. Open between 9am to 2am, seven days a week. Tel. 513112 p85.

CHAMPERS — Seafood restaurant has brought a fresh dimension to dining out at Oura. While specialising in fish and shellfish dishes, there is also meat on the menu. CHAMPERS' decor and unobtrusive background music is as pleasing to eye and ear as the food is to the palate. Open from 6.30 pm every day. Tel: 513074. p85.

ALBUFEIRA

Transport facilities

AUTO CERRO - An English Car Hire with the latest models. Small and larger cars available. Both service and attention given are very good. Tel: (089) 586425/6/7 - Telex: 56240 AUCERR P Fax: (089) 586428 P92, C12.

AVIS, Rua da Igreja Nova, 13. Tel: 52678 Hotel Dom Pedro. Touring Club - Aldeia das Açoteias. Tel: 50226. Telex: 56737 P. *P92, C14*

BUDGET RENT-A-CAR. Cerro Grande. Tel: 54997/53464. Telex: 56268 P. P92, C.

EUROPCAR INTERNACIONAL - Aluguer de Automoveis, Lda. Rua Dr. Diogo Leote. Tel: 512444-512411 Fax: 586400. Telex 58209.

AUTO JARDIM RENT-A-CAR. The largest portuguese Rent-a-Car. **Head Office**: Av. da Liberdade, Edifício Brisa, 8200 Albufeira. Tel: (089) 589715. Telex: 56203, Fax: (089) 513924. Lisbon: Tel: (01) 8514871, Telex: 60304. P92 C7.

Travel

DELTA TRAVEL AGENTS. This agency is run by an experienced travel professional whose staff can handle all your travel needs. They can organise rental cars, excursions, air trips, coach tours, tickets etc. With speed and efficiency. Open 9.30-6.30 every day except Sunday. Bullring.

TAGUS TRAVEL. A 30 year old agency whose departments provide all requirements for a full travel service, such as congresses, incentives, holiday travel, business travel, and youth travel. Head Office: R. Camilo Castelo Branco 20, 1100 Lisboa. Oporto Office: R. St.ª Catarina 661/3, Loja C, 4000 Porto, Algarve Branch Office: Algarve: Arcadas de S. João, Loja AE/BN - Areias de S. João - 8200 Albufeira - Telef.: (089) 586326/7 - Telex: 56911 TAGUS Fax: 586329.

Shopping

INFANTE D. HENRIQUE HOUSE, A fine selection of excellent quality Portuguese earthenware of XVII century design. Hand-made porcelain baskets (wickerwork-style). Now in stock, beautiful porcelain dishes in vegetable shapes. Rua Cândido dos Reis, 30. Tel: 53267. *P92, D40*

CHARLES JOURDAN at ST. JAMES, This leading shoe shop is the exclusive Algarve stockist of the world famous brand of shoes from Paris. At local prices! Av. 25 de Abril, Edificio TURlAL (near the Fisherman's beach). Tel: 515897. *P92, H5*

ISABEL'S, Once a beauty salon now with a brand new perfume store. Dna. Isabel with years of experience knows the needs of the shopper. Av. Eduardo Rios, 11. Tel: 586827. *P92, D42.*

VILA MAGNA SH0PPING CENTRE A large shopping centre in the Algarve on the ground floor and basement of Villa Magna Aparthotel, Montechoro. Bars, restaurants, boutiques, supermarket, cinema, discotheque and dozens of shops. Private parking.

SUPERMARKET MARRACHINHO. Algarve's famous supermarket with a wide selection of national and imported foods and drinks. English spoken. Located in the Cerro Grande development. *P92 C.*

Algarve's best value International Shopping Centre.

This large shopping centre is a few minutes walk from the centre of Albufeira and is also very well situated for those arriving by car, since it lies above the town near the main Albufeira bypass and very close to the proposed route of the Via Infante, the Algarve's soon-to-be completed new major road. Since its opening it has been an immediate success, owned as it is by a subsidiary of Sonae, one of Portugal's biggest industrial holding companies. The company's size and expertise has meant that they have attracted some top quality international and national retail chains into the centre. Altogether there are 65 shops in the centre, and visitors to the Algarve will find it a blessing. Here you can park easily 3000 cars, shop in air-conditioned comfort and security, and fulfill all your shopping needs under one roof. The Prisunic supermarket offers the cheapest food prices in the Algarve for self-catering visitors or those seeking wine and food to take home. For gifts there are several shops specialising in jewellery, giftware, paintings, silverware and you can develop your films and wash your clothes. The bank can exchange travellers cheques, and foreign newspapers are on sale in the newsagents. And, if you have a yearning for foreign food, try the Pizza Hut (open 11am - 12pm) and the croissant shops.

Located on the Albufeira bypass, near the Town Hall. Open 10am to 10pm seven days a week.

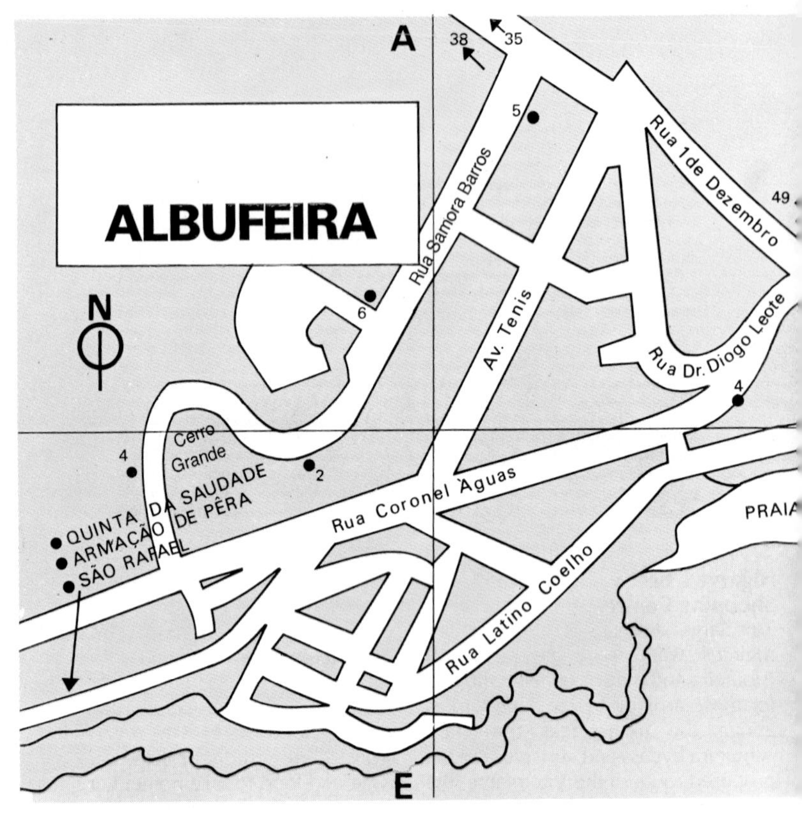

KEY TO MAP

Accommodation:

Aparthotel Jardim	C38
Club Albufeira	C57
Hotel Baltum	H1
Hotel Boa Vista	C
Hotel Sol e Mar	G3
Hotel da Aldeia	page 87
Cerro Grande	C
Est. Cerro	C
Carlton Hotel	page 88

Bars:

Caves do Vinho do Porto	C8

Car Rentals:

Auto Cerro	C12
Auto Jardim	C7
Budget	C
Avis	C14
Guérin	C16
RN Tours	D60
Europcar	page 91

Cinema	D17
Hospital	G18

Markets:

Fish	H19
Vegetables	C20
Post Office	C25

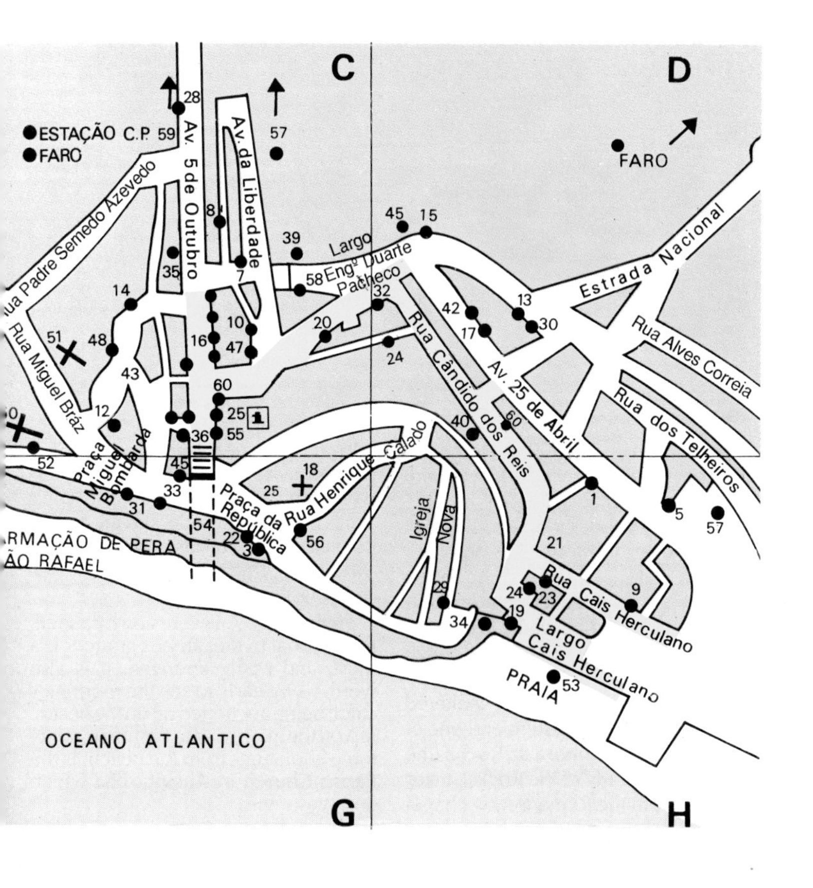

Restaurants:

Borda d'Água	page 90
Cabaz da Praia	G31
Jardim d'Allah	G22
Grill Boa Vista	C
Ruína	H34

Shopping:

Marrachinho (Supermarket)	C
Charles Jourdan at St. James	H5
Infante D. Henrique House	D40
Prisunic shopping Centre	page 91
Isabels	D42

Sightseeing:

Church Santana	C49
Church São Sebastião	C50
Church Matriz	C51
Fishermen's Beach	H53
Tunnel	G54
Tourist Office	C55
Town Hall	G56

Transportation:

Bus	C57
Taxi	C58
Train Station	C59

ARMAÇÃO DE PÊRA (44 kms from Faro Airport)

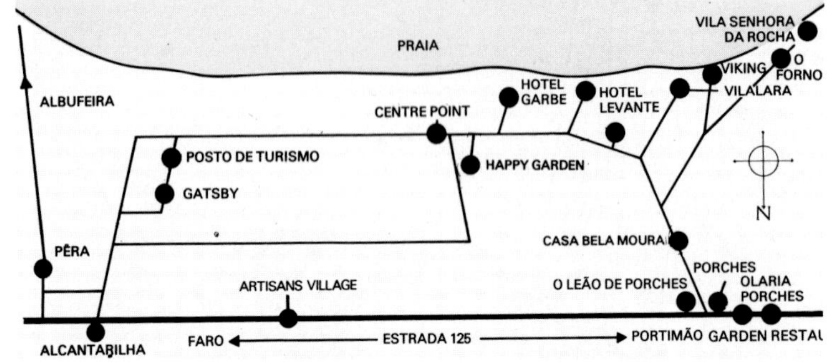

This fishing village lies some 40 kilometres west of Faro and lays claim to the largest beach in the whole of the Algarve. It is wide, sandy and safe. Set among huge sandstone cliffs and rock formations, the village is close to the ruins of an eighteenth century fort whose small chapel, dedicated to St. Anthony, is worthy of attention. Rock formations reaching down to the seashore form a series of sheltered beaches and at the western end one of these, the **Praia Senhora da Rocha** (the beach of Our Lady of the Rocks), takes its name from the Romanesque chapel which is perched, seemingly precariously, above it. Immediately west of this beach the sea has carved a series of caverns, vaults and grottoes in the area of Furnas. These caves **(Mesquita, Ruazes, Pontal)** are well worth visiting.

Sightseeing. An excursion by a small fishing boat to the famous grottoes is a must, and easily arranged. It is also worth rising early to see the morning's catch being auctioned off on the beach. Just off the main road to Portimão, some three kilometres from the beach, is the **Parish Church of Alcantarilha** which deserves a visit.

Accommodation

Hotel Garbe

HOTEL GARBE (****) One of Algarve's best known hotels, the Hotel Garbe has 120 rooms and 20 suites. All rooms are beautifully decorated, with direct dial phone, hairdryers, airconditioning, and private bathrooms. Now owned by the Baron Hotel Group from the United Kingdom. The restaurant serves Portuguese and international dishes, and there is also a coffee shop, and two bars which offer regular live music and other entertainments. The pool bar serves snacks. The hotel is superbly located on the cliffs with an unbroken view of the coast and direct access to the beach. Dining room and bars overlook the cliffs. There are also 2 conference rooms and a hairdresser. Contact the hotel on, Tel: (082) 312187/8, 312194/5 Telex: 58590 Fax: (082) 312201.

CASA BELA MOURA COUNTRY INN. Two rustic houses of recognised architectural merit - 12 bedrooms with private bath - 1 apartment with private entrance - swimming pool - loungebar roof-terraces - solarium - garden - car park. Professional family management. Address: Alporchinhos Road Armação de Pêra - Porches, 8635 Armação de Pêra. Tel: (082) 313025/313422 Telex: 58726 Fax: 351 (082) 313025.

Also visit the Hotel Levante (Salvor Hotels) see page 107.

Restaurants - Bars

O GATSBY. A lovely popular restaurant bar. Specialities include "Lombo a Gatsby", Fillet Steak in butter cream and brandy, Veal Escalopes in wine sauce, Port and Clams in Wine, Scampi in Wine and Tomato Sauce. Also wide variety of other meat, fish and seafood dishes. Rua Dr. Manuel d'Arriaga, 109. Tel: 813535. Open for dinner only.

THE HAPPY GARDEN . Peking cuisine. Specialities pork piquant, sweet & sour chicken, peking duck. Open for lunch and dinner. Ibercentro, Torre Iberius.

PORCHES. A small village on the way to Lagoa.

Shopping - Restaurants

OLARIA PEQUENA POTTERY Located on the main road (EN 125) directly opposite the turn-off for Porches and Armação de Pêra. This is a working pottery producing bright modern ceramics: handmade functional tableware and colourful decorative tiles. Well worth a visit! Open to the public Monday to Friday. Tel: 53213.

PORCHES

O LEÃO DE PORCHES. Internationally known for good food. This 17th century farmhouse in the centre of the ancient village of Porches is a most charming and intimate restaurant. Tel: 52384.

CASA ALGARVE — A delightful shop well stocked with a variety of Portuguese handicrafts and pottery. One range of ceramics is especially made for Mr Salvador Alves, the owner, and is exclusive to the shop. Here is the best range of handpainted wall friezes in the Algarve - displayed outside. Located west of Porches on the EN 125. Tel (082) 52682.

QUINTA DO ROSAL — The wooded estate is seven minutes from the lively market town of **Lagoa** with its restaurants, bars, shops and vineyards. All the villa plots at Quinta do Rosal have been carefully arranged to give a feeling of countryside seclusion while still benefiting from the facilities the development will offer, like a restaurant, bar, large swimming pool, tennis courts, shops, management and letting centre, maid and garden service, security and car hire. Ferreira and Gilpin Ldª, Rua 25 de Abril, 27 — 8400 LAGOA. Tel: (082) 53745-53681. Fax: (082) 53251.

SLIDE AND SPLASH. Slide and Splash is considered one of the best and safest aquatic leisure parks in Europe. It is a huge complex - 40,000 m2 of fun and fantasy. Among the water fun rides are 4 main slides, a Double Corkscrew, a Banzai Run, a Kamikaze Run, a Whirl Pool, a Water Fall, a River Ride, a Jumping Castle for children, diving and swimming areas, changing rooms and showers, restaurants, a giftshop and a first aid post. Slide and Splash is located within easy reach of Lagoa, Praia do Carvoeiro, and Praia da Rocha, with free parking. Hotel guests in the area can also be picked up by special buses. **For more information phone: (082) 341685 Fax: (082) 341826 Estrada Nacional 125, Vale de Deus, Estombar, 8400 Lagoa.**

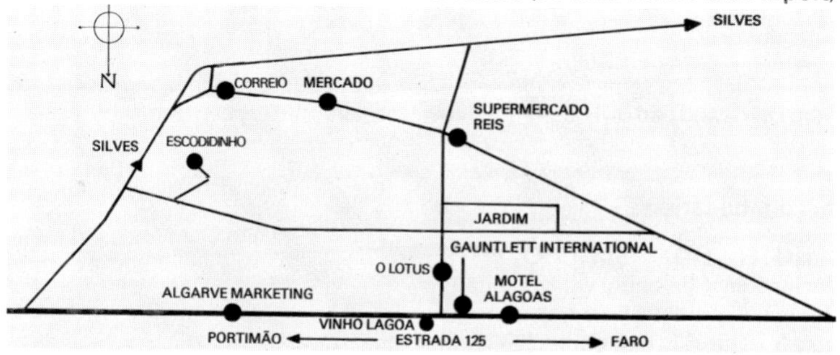

LAGOA A small and interesting town where the excellent Lagoa wine is produced. Tours can be arranged for visits to the winery at Lagoa.

Real Estate Opportunities

ALGARVE MARKETING - PROPRIEDADES, Lda. (Jan Frederick Luijt, Licensed real-estate and insurance agent): Real Estate Purchase and Sale; villa construction, maintenance and administration; all Insurances - home policies, car insurance, worker's compensation, personal accident policies. **Estrada Nacional 125/Km 51, Apartado 27, 8400 Lagoa. Tel: 082-52426; Telex 57498 ALMARK P; Telefax: (082) 52979.**

Restaurants

O LOTUS. Noted for the quality of their Portuguese cooking. Long established, comfortable. Facing GALP petrol station. Closed Saturdays. Tel: 52098.

Car hire

AVIS. Hotel do Levante, Tel: 52678, Telex: 56737.

CARVOEIRO

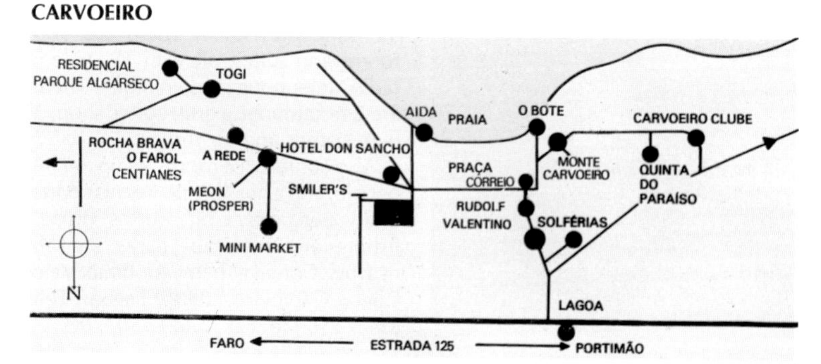

CARVOEIRO

Introduction

The village lies some five kilometres from Lagoa and part of its attraction lies in the secluded beaches, some of which may only be reached from the sea.

Accommodation

HOTEL DOM SANCHO (****) Located in Carvoeiro village square, the hotel is only 50 metres from the beach. The 51 bedrooms (23 with seaview) all have private bathrooms, radio, telephone and airconditioning. The restaurant serves English, French and Portuguese food. There are 2 swimming pools, (one has sun terraces and poolside bar serving snacks and salads), a TV/video lounge and regular live entertainment. Babysitting, car hire, laundry, and medical services are also all available. Owned by the Baron Hotel Group from the United Kingdom. Tel. (082) 357301/2/3/4/50, Fax: (082) 357211. Telex: 57472.

HOTEL ALMANSOR (****) Built within yards of the sea and the beach at Vale Covo, this magnificent hotel has spectacular views across its pools to the sand and cliffs. There are 400 rooms and suites, all with TV, video, radio, telephone and minibar. There are 2 restaurants, a grill, coffee shop, 3 bars, games and TV rooms.

Also conference rooms for up to 700 people, and a health club, tennis courts and watersports. Golf courses, riding, fishing and waterfun parks are all nearby. Contact them at Praia Vale Covo, Carvoeiro, 8400 Lagoa. Tel: (082) 358026, Fax: (082) 358770.

Accommodation

TOGI APARTMENTS for rental - 5 two room and 4 studios fully furnished, comfortable apartments, in a beautiful location next to Togi restaurant. Tel: 082-358517.

Restaurants

CENTIANES (Vale Centianes). A special place where Astrid and Alexander Wirthl are known for their Special Menus! Dinner only. Tel: 58724.

AIDA — Restaurant-Bar. Portuguese operated. Their speciality fresh fish and shellfish from their own tank! Located left side of Carvoeiro beach. Tel: 357396. (April-October).

GATO'S STONE STEAK — Recently redecorated, in the midst of the Monte Carvoeiro village, here the freshest fish and meat is cooked and served on stones. It's unique and delicious. Open every day for lunch and dinner and well worth a visit. Tel: (082) 357730.

TEODORO'S On the cliff overlooking the beach, this chic black and white restaurant offers the freshest seafood and fish, brought, from Portimão and Sagres, in seawater tanks. It seats 70 inside (with airconditioning) and 30 on the openair terrace. The service is first class, the meals very good value for money and Teodoro, the owner, is often there. Rampa Srª da Encarnação, Tel. (082) 357864.

TOGI. Located above Algar Seco, in luxurious garden surroundings. The tropical style dining room and bar makes relaxing pleasant, while waiting for tasty French or Portuguese cuisine specialities. Tel: 082-358517.

A REDE Cosy and inviting at the top of Estrada Farol. Their good choice of seafood (including swordfish) and tuna steaks) plus meat dishes, is varied. A lovely patio for warm evenings. Estrada do Farol. Tel: (082) 358513.

Travel.

AVIS — Rua do Barranco, 3 Tel.: 22029, Telex: 56737.

KENNING - Praia do Carvoeiro - c/o JG Agency - R. dos Pescadores, 1 - 8400 Lagoa - Tel. (082) 357311 - Tlx. 57623 Altime P - Fax (089) 818503.

SILVES (63 kms from Faro Airport)

Standing at the junction of the **Odelouca** and **Arade** rivers, some twenty kilometres north of Portimão, this city was the Moorish capital of the Algarve, being larger and far more important than Lisbon. Today it has some 20,000 inhabitants. Its decline began with its liberation from the Moors, but the worst blow came with the earthquake of 1755 which virtually destroyed the entire town. Fortunately the **Cathedral of Santa Maria** survived, though badly damaged. Built in the thirteenth century, it has the remnants of a Moorish mosque behind its altar and a fine doorway. On the Silves-Messines road is a sixteenth century stone lacework cross known as the **Cross of Portugal,** which should not be missed!

Sightseeing. A visit to the Barragem Arade, a dam set in the hills a short distance from Silves is a scenic and pleasant side trip to take. There is a restaurant and picnic area there.

Property

REAL ESTATE-DINAMICO LDA — A long established company (English) and Government - Licensed estate agent. In the old Moorish capital city of the Algarve, Silves. They deal in building land, villa construction, villa re-sales etc. And also have many large developments including golf courses, hotels and farms. 1 Rua da Sé, 8300 SILVES Tel. (082) 442718/442916 Fax (082) 443693.

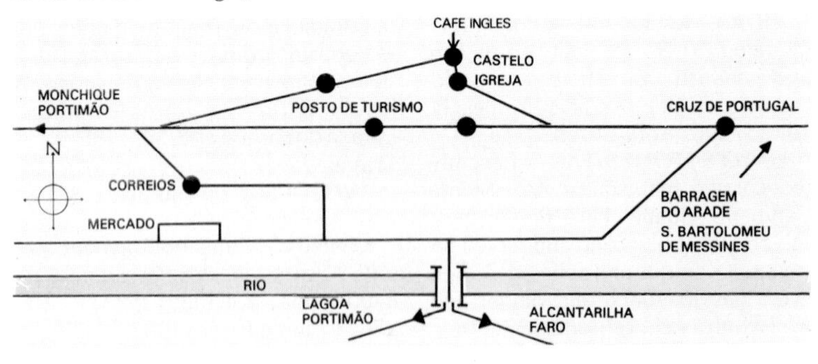

Ferragudo - Traditional Village near Portimão

Apart from being the busiest city along the Algarve coast, Portimão is also the largest. Although often compared with Faro, Portimão in fact is bigger, with more bustle and life. Soon life in the city will greatly improve with the completion of the bridge over the river Arade outside the town - which will ease traffic congestion and free the streets for pedestrians.

Alongside the old bridge into the town are the quays where dozens of boats unload their catches of tunny and sardines. It is thought that the town is built on the site of a Phoenician or Carthaginian trading post, and it was certainly known to the Romans.

Portimão is the best shopping city in the Algarve. Here are the shops of some of the area's most professional retailers who are accustomed to talk to clients, explain the stock and make sure they leave satisfied. The town also has a large pedestrian area always full of streetlife, restaurants and people. One thing all visitors must do - eat freshly grilled sardines overlooking the harbour. Aah, the smell and the taste of Portugal!

PORTIMÃO

Restaurants/Bars

A LANTERNA - Portuguese operated. Specialise in seafood. Very good as Sr. Baptista the owner has been catering for years in the Algarve. Their smoked swordfish and fish soup is a must. Prices reasonable. Located just across the Portimão Bridge (Ferragudo side). Tel: 23948. (Closed Sundays). *P99, H26.*

O GATO. On a par with any top quality Portuguese restaurant, the decor and furnishings are most attractive. Portuguese and international cuisine. Well recommended. Located at the beginning of the road leading to Alvor Praia. Tel:27674 P113

O BUQUE - Experienced Portuguese caterers. Excellent Portuguese cuisine.'Cataplanas' are their speciality. Dark wooden beams - most attractive decor. Spacious lower floor with large bar ideal for parties. Located right-side main road before Portimão river bridge. Tel: 24678 *P99, H44.*

O BICHO — A large airy restaurant serving typical Portuguese food, the freshest fish grilled, stews, seafood and local vegetables. Very good value, and very friendly staff. Closed on Sundays. Largo Gil Eanes, 12. Tel: (082) 22977.

AVÓZINHA - Well recommended as specialists in all types of shell fish (live), cataplanas, and always fresh fish. Rua do Capote. Tel: 22922 (Closed Tuesdays). P99, G15

SIMSA RESTAURANT - A nice cosy restaurant, and the food is something different. International cuisine with oriental flavours, cooked by the proprietor herself. Very well worth a visit. Closed Sundays. Reservations recommended. Contact Inge and Harry. Rua São Gonçalo, 7. Tel. (082) 23057. *P99, C20*

Shopping

Near the market and main church is the principal shopping street closed to traffic, **Rua do Comércio.** Another most interesting shopping street is **Rua Sta. Isabel**. Here the shops specialise in Portuguese handicrafts, art, crystal, glass, fashion and leather.

BAZAR-MIRIAMIS. If you wish to take from Portugal a remembrance of its crafts here is a well stocked shop. Will mail or ship to all parts. Largo do Dique, *11. P98, F28.*

CHARCUTARIA BALAIO - (Delicatessen) - With Portuguese and foreign produce: large variety of sausages; cheese; take-away food; wines - wide selection of foodstuff. Rua do Comercio 8. Tel: 23215. P98, B23

SUPERMARKET ALVORADA. English spoken, considered to be one of the best for its wide selection of groceries and drinks, local and imported (special offers). Rua Diogo Gonçalves. Tel. 22700. *P98, B*

CASCO GARRAFEIRA. An excellent and beautifully organised store carrying ample stocks of all manner of wines, liqueurs, spirits and other drinks of all kinds. The wine tasting bar is most attractive and inviting! Rua João de Deus 24, extension of Avenida João de Deus. Tel: 23044. *P 99, C11.*

CHARLES JOURDAN at ST. JAMES. This leading shoe shop is the exclusive Algarve stockist of the world famous brand of shoes from Paris. At local prices! Rua Sta. Isabel, 26. Portimão (near the harbour). Tel: 24620. *P99, G33.*

GABY'S. Specialists in high quality leather goods, crocodile, snake skin goods, Rua Direita, 5 and Praça Visconde Bívar, 15 Tel: 411988 F24 and G24.

CONFORTALIS FURNITURE - One of the Algarve's better shops for variety and quality. Their two shops, located very close to one another, have among other items on display hand built bamboo furniture and hand painted furniture for which Portugal is noted. Tel: (082) 24200. Rua do Comércio, 39 and Rua Hortinha, 19. Tel: (082) 24200. Fax: (082) 411883. *P99, C31 G49.*

VINDA BOUTIQUE. Browse through five rooms of this unique shop in an old former private residence. The finest in Portuguese pewter and ovenproof pottery. One-of-a-kind women's fashions, custom designed by David Browne of New York. Also handknit sweaters and dresses. Madeira embroideries in blouses, children's wear, table linens, handkerchiefs, etc. Recommended by VOGUE, GOURMET, Fielding's Guide. Rua Santa Isabel 32. Tel: 23373. *P99 G 38.*

Three shops to visit (see page 38) - all managed by the same family - on Praça da Republica, Rua Vasco da Gama, 41 and Rua Direita.

O AQUARIO. Operated by a young Portuguese couple with taste who have filled their shop with a wide variety of ATLANTIS CRYSTAL GLASS, VISTA ALEGRE PORCELAIN, HAND PAINTED CERAMICS and beautiful pewter items. They are near the market on the corner of **Rua Vasco da Gama and Praca da Republica. Tel: 26673** ***P98, B26***

O AQUARIO II. The only specialist shop in the Algarve for handmade articles made in copper, bronze, pewter, finest hand painted ceramics, and superb marble collection. **Rua Vasco da Gama, 41.** ***P98,B27***

O AQUARIO III. Spacious, excellent for quality ceramics, porcelain and crystal for the home or gifts. Beautifully displayed. **Rua Direita, Loja 10 Tel: 414195** ***P98, B21***

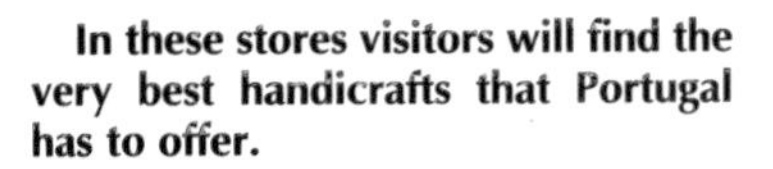

In these stores visitors will find the very best handicrafts that Portugal has to offer.

Algarve's Biggest shopping Centre

This huge shopping centre is the sister to the very successful Prisunic Shopping Centre in Albufeira. This one, however, is even larger!

Located well outside the crowded narrow streets of the city centre, it lies on the EN 124 in the direction of Praia de Rocha at the corner of Av. Miguel Bombarda. Even better, there is parking for 2500 cars a day. The centre, with its permanent security facilities for the protection of cars and shoppers has revolutionised shopping in Portimão for residents and visitors alike. In total there are two floors, linked by easy access rolling pavements, large elevators and escalators. Apart from the huge Prisunic supermarket on the ground floor, there are 150 other shops, ranging from internationally known brand names like The Sweet Factory, Boticário, Nectar, Uniform, Esprit and Pizza Hut to famous Portuguese retail chains of shoes and clothes shops. There are also several shops that cater to everyday needs (bank, chemist, etc.) and shops where you can purchase holiday gifts. Most importantly, here visitors can find the most competitive food prices in the Algarve, ideal for those in self-catering apartments or who are spending long periods of time here. To take a break from shopping, you can also eat at any one of a number of small good value restaurants located in the centre. Well worth a visit for your shopping needs. Pizza Hut is open 11 am - 12 pm.

Located on EN 124 at corner with Avenida Miguel Bombarda on the road out to Praia da Rocha. Open 10am to 10pm seven days a week.

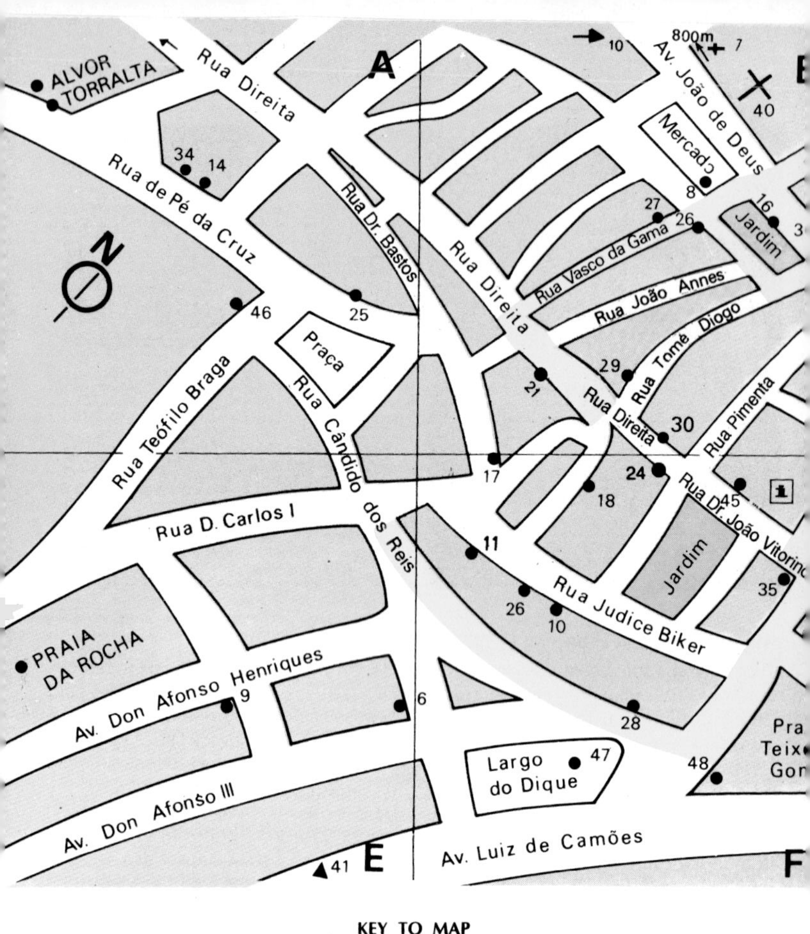

KEY TO MAP

Accommodation:		**Restaurants:**	
Hotel Globo	G1	Avózinha	G15
Car Rentals:		A Lanterna	H26
Avis-Praia da Rocha-Torralta		Mariners	G34
Cinema	E6	O Gato	Page 102
Hospital	B7	O Bicho	D60
Market	B8	O Buque	H44
Post Office	E9	Simsa	C20
Real Estate:		**Bars:**	
Evans Realsol	F11	Mariners	G34

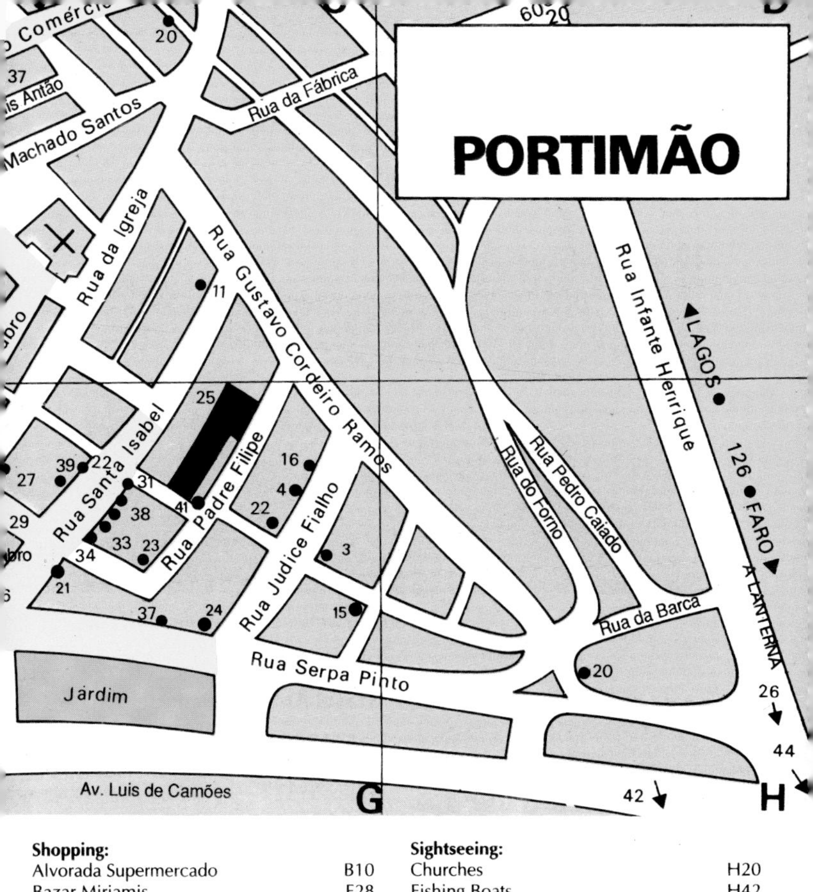

Shopping:

Alvorada Supermercado	B10
Bazar Miriamis	F28
O Casco Garrafeira	C11
Charcutaria Balaio	B23
Confortalis	C31 G49
Gaby's - Leather	F24 G24
O Aquário	B26
O Aquário II	B27
O Aquário III Rua Direita	B21
Shoes Charles Jourdan at St. James	G33
Vinda Boutique	G38
Oliveira's Joalheiros	G37
Modelo Prisunic	Page 103
Vista Alegre	G39

Sightseeing:

Churches	H20
Fishing Boats	H42

Tourist Office	F45
Town Hall	A46

Transportation:

Bus	F47
Taxi	B16 F48
Train	D50

Travel Agencies:

Agência Abreu	D51
RN Tours	F10
Star	F24

Ferragudo beach opposite Portimão

Real estate and rental opportunities

JOHN R EVANS - REALSOL LDA. (Government approved agents). Have on their books a large variety of properties well worth viewing, including villas, apartments, building plots, large land areas for urbanisation investments and business. Rua Judice Biker, 35. Tel: 26206/28889. Fax: 24765 Telex: 57309 *P98 F11*.

Travel Arrangements

STAR TRAVEL SERVICE - Rua Júdice Biker 26-A. Tel: (082) 2503 Telex:57312
P98 F24

AGENCIA ABREU. Founded in Oporto in 1840. Still managed by direct descendants who decided to add to their network of 20 offices, located in various parts of the world, yet another office in the Algarve, specialising in Groups, Incentives, Congresses and Seminars, in order to offer their clients their utmost assistance. Portimão: R. Infante D. Henrique, 83, 8500 Portimão. Tel: (351.82) 416151 Fax: (351.82) 416258 Telex: 57332.

This is one of the most famous resorts of the entire Algarve coast, and owes its origins to the wealthy citizens of Portimão who built villas there at the beginning of this century. It has a fine situation some two kilometres from Portimão and its beaches are divided by huge and weirdly shaped rocks. These dominate the splendid sandy beach and have many natural passages and arches. A long promenade runs on the clifftop above the beach, and it is here that the villas, hotels and other establishments are to be found, giving Praia da Rocha its 'international' flavour. Excellent views may be had from the old Fortress **of Sta Catarina**, and the cliff path of the rich gold sand and the dull red of the rocks against the sapphire-coloured sea.

Sightseeing. A trip to the nearby beaches of **Vau**, **Praia de Alvor** and **Praia de Carvoeiro** can be made by sea or road. Other sightseeing trips may be arranged at your hotel.

Accommodation.

HOTEL JÚPITER (****) 180 rooms all with private bath and most with balcony, very attractive decor in lounges, two restaurants, cosy bar and coffee shop. Swimming pool - heated and covered in winter, shops and night club. Located near the beach. Cable Júpiterotel, Praia da Rocha. Tel: 415041/5. Telex: 57346 Fax: 415319.

HOTEL AVENIDA PRAIA (***) A new modern, attractive 61 bedroom hotel, all with private bath and balcony with beach and sea views. Two bars, breakfast room and TV, garage and solarium. Av. Tomás Cabreira, Praia da Rocha. Tel: (082) 85872/3/4. Telex: 56448 P

HOTEL ORIENTAL (****) This spectacular new aparthotel, of authentic moorish design, sits on the cliffs overlooking the sea and beach.

Surrounded by gardens, terraces, and swimming pools, the rooms are luxuriously decorated, with TV, phones and safes. There is also a sauna, hairdresser, bars and large conference rooms. The hotel is restful and relaxed, and well worth a visit. Tel: (082) 413000. Fax: (082) 413413. Telex: 58788.

HOTEL ALGARVE (*****) 220 rooms with full bath, frigo-bar in all rooms, air conditioning and a large covered balcony with a magnificent view of the sea. The decor of the hotel facilities is very much Moorish in the lounges, bridge room and bar. The two salt water swimming pools are beautifully set on the cliff's edge overlooking the beach. Other amenities: garden, mini-golf, solarium, shops, bank, hairdresser, barber and a health centre. Beach facilities with bar, 2 tennis courts, snack bar with Portuguese dishes.

For reservations at the hotel etc. Tel: (082) 235001. Cable Algarvotel, Praia da Rocha. Telex: 57347 ALOTEL P. Telefax: (082) 235999 (Full convention facilities up to 120 persons.) *P110.*

PRAIA DA ROCHA

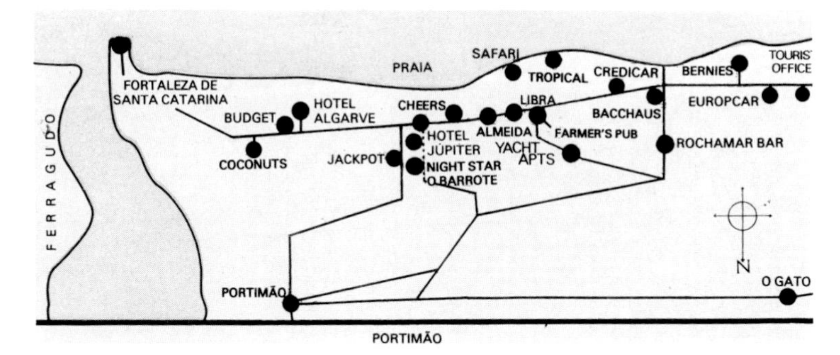

Restaurants - Bars

BACCHUS BAR PUB. The owner, a professional bartender for years, knew the ropes when he set up his place. The open air esplanade is most pleasant. Very good for a drink and food. Up from the Hotel Tarik.

BENNIES PIZZA AND CREPE. Bennie has 'line ups' from when he first opens in the morning until the evening. Once having eaten here you will know why. His food is great, yet reasonably priced. Av. Tomaz Cabreira.

TROPICAL BEACH. For a wonderful evening watching the sunset over the beach! Álvaro, the chef-owner creates superb dishes with attention to detail. The avocado stuffed with chicken, tamboril, kebab or fish stew are wonderful examples. Come early for a seat with a view. Areal, Praia da Rocha. Tel: 26738.

SAFARI. Portuguese operated. Noted for fish, chicken curry and charcoal grills. However, there are other house specialities with an African touch. Rua António Feu. Tel: 24540. Reservations recommended.

O BARROTE - Restaurant and Pub. Pleasant, cosy ambience for an excellent meal or drink. Service a la carte. Located in Hotel Jupiter's shopping area. Tel: 235041.

NIGHT STAR CLUB. One of the Algarve's most elegant discotheques. Located in Hotel Jupiter, Praia da Rocha. Tel: 245041/8.

Hotels ALGARVE, JUPITER, ALVOR and **Torralta ADEGA - ALVOR CASINO,** are also good for dancing

Transport Facilities - Travel

AVIS. Outer Galleries. Telex: 56737 P. Hotel Algarve, Tel: 245029.

BUDGET RENT-A-CAR. Av. Tomaz Cabreira. Tel: 245370.

EUROPCAR INTERNACIONAL. Aluguer de Automoveis, Lda. Av. Tomás Cabreira, Edificio Belo Horizonte. Tel: 24465/24114/5. Fax: 411941.

MILTOURS Travel agents, Group operator. Praia da Rocha. Office: Edificio Marivau Loja 1 Tel: 82798 . Telex: 56798 Fax: 84342. Head office in Faro R. Veríssimo de Almeida 14, Tel.:

KENNING - Praia da Rocha - Hotel da Rocha - 8500 Portimão Tel: (082) 23392 - Telex: 56781 Kenfar P - Fax: (089) 818503.

MONCHIQUE (89 kms from Faro Airport)

The hills of Monchique are the setting for one of the most interesting excursions to be made in the Algarve. Viewsaremagnificent and cool breezes provide a relaxing contrast to the heat of the coast in mid-summer. The small village of **Caldas de Monchique** is a delightful stopover point and a must for a visit. Some of the 17th century buildings have been restored to their original elegance and house many amenities: an **inn, restaurant**, **bar**, **handicraft shop** and a **'bouvette'** for drinking the famous Monchique spa water. The therapeutic value of **Termas das Caldas de Monchique** dates back to the time of the Romans.

Restaurants.

PARAISO DA MONTANHA. One of the most popular and typical restaurants of the area specialising in chicken piripiri and excellent sliced ham. Spacious. Good regional sweets. 3kms from Monchique on the **Foia** road. Tel: 92150. (Closed Thursdays).

TERESINHA. Comfortable restaurant with views over the valley and the background coastline from Portimão to Lagos. Closed Monday. Regional dishes with chicken and codfish 'Bacalhau à Teresinha', sliced ham and regional sweets. On the **Foia** road. Tel: 92392.

BICA-BOA "INN". Restaurant/Bar. Lisbon Road 1km from Monchique. Very beautiful setting. Tastefully decorated by Irish/Portuguese owners. Original menu. Bed and breakfast with full facilities. Splash pool, terrace, attractive garden. Tel: 92271. Telex: 57443 FOIA P.

ALVOR

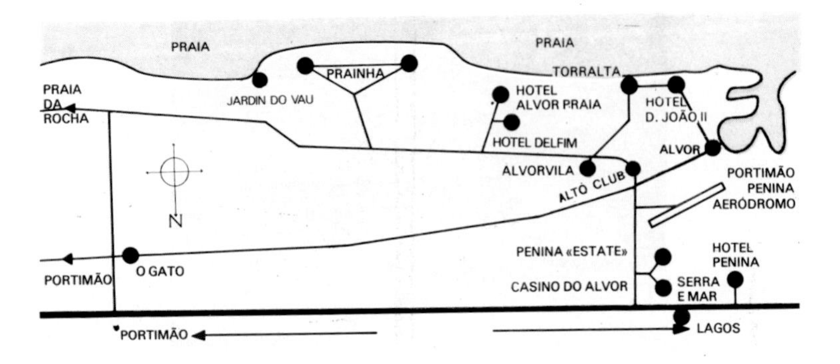

THE ALTO CLUB

Masterminded by John Stilwell, (one of the pioneers of Algarve tourism with his development of the Penina estates and golf course in the 1960s), the Alto Club property development near Alvor is located in 18 picturesque acres looking down across the bay of Lagos. The development is offering 3 types of Algarvean-style property, together with membership of the Henry Cotton designed golf course currently being built nearby. Buyers can either purchase 1-6 weeks a year in the designer-furnished apartments (and become members of an international timeshare exchange scheme into the bargain) or luxury detached villas with swimming pools.

There is also the superb Alto Club restaurant. For more information contact **Alto Club, Apartado 1, Alvor, 8500 Portimão. Tel: (082) 459119, or Almond Leisure, Crusader House, 14 Pall Mall, London SW1, (071) 839 4121, England.**

Alvor

Accomodation

HOTEL ALVOR-PRAIA (*****) This is the famous beach resort hotel with 199 completely refurbished rooms, and 18 elegant suites. All rooms are airconditioned, with full bathroom, hairdryer, radio, satelite TV and direct dial telephone. 160 ocean view rooms have a balcony. The hotel is located on low sandstone cliffs, overlooking the beaches, ocean and the bay of Lagos. Apart from direct beach access, the hotel offers boutiques, hairdressers, snack and cocktail bars, the exclusive Grill restaurant that serves international and Portuguese cuisine to live piano music, and other snack and cocktail bars. There are also conference rooms, a cinema and rent-a-car facilities. Sports on offer include a heated pool, tennis courts, putting green, volley ball, nearby horseriding, sauna, massages and pedicures. Guests have a 30% green fee discount at the famous nearby golfcourses. Its a true five star hotel. **Tel. (082) 458900, Fax: (082) 458999.**

HOTEL DELFIM (****) Near the Alvor Praia Hotel, this 312 room hotel is famous for its friendly service and atmosphere. All the rooms are air conditioned, have full bathroom, satelite TV, radio and direct dial telephone. There is a large seawater pool. Apart from the hotel's restaurants and shops there is tennis (7 courts), tabletennis, volleyball, watersports and a health club. Guests get a 30% green fee reduction at the nearby golf courses. **Tel: (082) 458901 Fax: (082) 458970**

Hotel Alvor Praia
Hotel Delfim
Hotel Dom João
Hotel Golfinho
Hotel do Levante
Golf Country Club
Vilamoura

ALGARVE AT ITS BEST

HOTEL DOM JOÃO (****). This 220 room hotel is on the Alvor beach and ideal for families. All rooms have satelite TV and direct dial phone, and the hotel has a heated pool, grillroom and restaurant. Nearby attractions include the Casino de Rocha, golf courses with greenfee discounts and many sports options; tennis, bowling, tabletennis and watersports.
Tel: (082)459135/6/7 Fax: (082) 459363 Telex: 57321.

Hotel Alvor Praia

HOTEL GOLFINHO (****) Situated near Lagos, this 262 room hotel is only 200m from Praia Dona Ana, a famous Algarve cove. All rooms have satelite TV, and there are bars, discos and restaurants in the hotel. The disco is particularly well known. The pool is heated and covered in winter, and there is a bowling alley. **Tel: (082) 769900. Telex: 57497 HotgolP Fax: (082) 769999.**

HOTEL DO LEVANTE (****) Near the village of Armação de Pêra, this 41 room hotel is like a private house. All rooms have satelite TV, and direct dial telephone, and there are 2 bars and a restaurant. A large seawater pool, minigolf, tabletennis, and nearby golf courses with green fee discounts are all offered.
Tel: (082) 314900 Fax: (082) 314903 Telex: 57478 P.

Car Hire

AUTO CERRO. Edifício Alvormar - ALVOR, 8500 PORTIMÃO, Tel: (082) 458274/458564

PENINA GOLF AND RESORT HOTEL (*****). Set in secluded countryside, the hotel provides all manner of activities. The huge pool has its own restaurant or you can use the hotel's private beach served by regular private bus (5 minutes away). There you will find a beach restaurant and watersports, and back at the hotel there are 8 tennis courts, horse riding, Penina Jeeps for your use, 2 golf courses and, of course, the international Championship Golf Course (18 holes) that surrounds the hotel. The recently-introduced "Penguin Village" is a supervised fun centre for children who have their own pool, zoo and restaurant. The hotel also has several very special restaurants. There is the Penina Grill which serves the freshest, most traditional Portuguese cooking, and the Harlequin, which serves authentic Italian dishes. The Monchique bar offers live music and the ideal place to unwind after dinner. There are also saunas, massages, a hairdresser, and car hire.

Each room has private bath, airconditioning, telephone, radio, TV, 24 hours room service and a private bar on request. Conference rooms with space for 600 people are available. For information call: (082) 415415. Fax: (082) 415000. Telex: 57307/57325.

A TRUSTHOUSE FORTE HOTEL

LAGOS (78 kms from Faro Airport)

With its deep water harbour and wide bay, Lagos is a fascinating and historic town. At the time of Moorish occupation, it was the centre for trade between Portugal and Africa. Its shipyards built the caravels which sailed on voyages of exploration made by Henry the Navigator's captains. In Nelson's day, British fleets were frequent visitors to its superb bay. In the old part of the town the visitor may still see sections of the early Roman walls and admire the ancient fortress which guards the harbour. Also to be seen in Lagos is the site of the first **slave market** to be established in Europe, and close to it, the former palace of **Dom Henrique**, now a hospital. The **Chapel of St. António**, a superb example of Portuguese eighteenth century baroque, is also worth seeing, with its gilded wood carvings and paintings. So ornate is the carving that the chapel is known as the 'Golden Chapel'. To the South of the town is the promontory with several fine beaches. Lagos is a busy fishing port and the town's main street runs beside the estuary quaysides.

Sightseeing. A day trip to nearby grottoes may be arranged through the tourist office. At an isolated beach sardines are grilled and local wine is served.

Apart from the walls which surround the town and the Golden Chapel of St. António (mentioned above) the church of San Sebastião with its lateral Renaissance door is also worth a visit. There are museums in Lagos too, the Museum of Ethnography, Archaeology, Numismatology, and Sacred Art are located in the Church of St. António. A great variety of Roman ruins are still to be seen, as well as an interesting aquaduct from the sixteenth century.

LAGOS

Accommodation

APARTHOTEL MEIA PRAIA BEACH CLUB, owned by the Dom Pedro Hotel Group, and 2 kilometres from Lagos, this aparthotel is only 100 metres from the beach. 83 apartments, with kitchens, telephones, colour TV and fridge make it an ideal selfcatering centre. The aparthotel also has games rooms, nearby watersports and special discounts at all the local golfcourses. **Lagos.** Tel: (082) 60951. Telex: 56788.

Hotel Golfinho - see page 107

Restaurants

D. SEBASTIÃO. Portuguese operated. Here it is possible to enjoy certain specialities; regional dishes, charcoal grills, shell-fish (live) and a wide variety of aged wines. Rua 25 de Abril, 20-22. Tel: 62795. P112, *E30*

O GALEÃO. Operated by young Portuguese Swiss-trained chefs. Very good regional and international cuisine. Fun to watch the 'busy scene' through the open kitchen. Reservations recommended. Rua da Laranjeira, 1 - Tel: 63909. P112, *B31*

O TROVADOR is something special! Its unique food and friendly atmosphere and the warm hospitality offered by Marion and Dave are a big plus. Open daily (except Sunday and Monday) from 19.00. A few yards up the hill behind Hotel Lagos. Tel: 63152. *P113, H17*

POUSO DO INFANTE. Portuguese operated. A sailing boat decor with beams of ships of old. Good variety of dishes. Tel: 62862. P120, *F26.*

CARDÁPIO - It is great to see a Portuguese family running their own restaurant. Charcoal grills and regional dishes are their specialities and prices are reasonable. Top end of Rua 25 Abril, 79. Tel: 61330.*P112 F24*

LAGOS COUNTRY CLUB, On a hill overlooking the town of Lagos. This club has a very special restaurant, and also offers 7 well equipped bungalows, a swimming pool, a snooker room, bowling green (which is very rare in the Algarve) and a barbecue area. Many local residents are club members in order to benefit from the facilities. The restaurant serves beautifully prepared, very reasonably priced lunches and dinners.

The dishes are original and use only the freshest local produce. Follow the signs as you leave Lagos on the E.N. 125 heading for Portimão. Apartado 106, 8600 Lagos. Tel: (082) 62060. *P113 H44*

Sports.

Sailing, water skiing, tennis, swimming, fishing (angling and underwater). Facilities for water skiing and sailing - contact your hotel desk or the local tourist office. The yacht harbour is good, but does present a tidal problem - boats become beached at low tide.

Transportation facilities

AVIS. Largo das Portas de Portugal, 11. Tel: 63691. Telex: 56737 P.

EUROPCAR INTERNACIONAL - Aluguer de Automoveis Lda. Estrada Nacional 120, Lote 1. Tel: 63173-63203 Fax: 767567.

KENNING Lagos - PMS - R. Vasco da Gama, 42-A - Tel. 63906

Real Estate and rental opportunities.

JILL LLOYD. Govt. Licensed Estate Agents offers a large selection of apartments, small villas and luxury villas with pool for short term rentals and sale in Praia da Luz and Lagos. Rua da Praia 23. Tel: Lagos (082) 789359, Fax: (082) 789908. Telex: 57600 LLOYDA P.

SADLER & MOREIRA LDA. Long established local estate agents with re-sale villas in Luz Bay Club, Luz Ocean Club and individual villas in the western Algarve. Tel: (082) 789336 or Fax: 789641.

LUZ BAY CLUB Occupying the Prime Location in the village overlooking the safe sandy beach. Villas and apartments and studios to rent for long and short term. Very reasonable winter rates. All enquiries: Luz Bay Club, Rua Direita 102, Praia da Luz, Tel: (082) 789640/ 789645, Fax: (082) 789641, Telex: 57661 LUZBAY P.

KEY TO MAP

Accommodation:

Hotel Meia Praia East of Lagos Page 117

Car Rentals:

Contauto H10
Guérin G14

Post Office G18

Cinema B12
Hospital E13
Market G14

Night Spots:

Clube Lançarote A15

Restaurants:

Alpendre B21
D. Sebastião F30
O Galeão B31

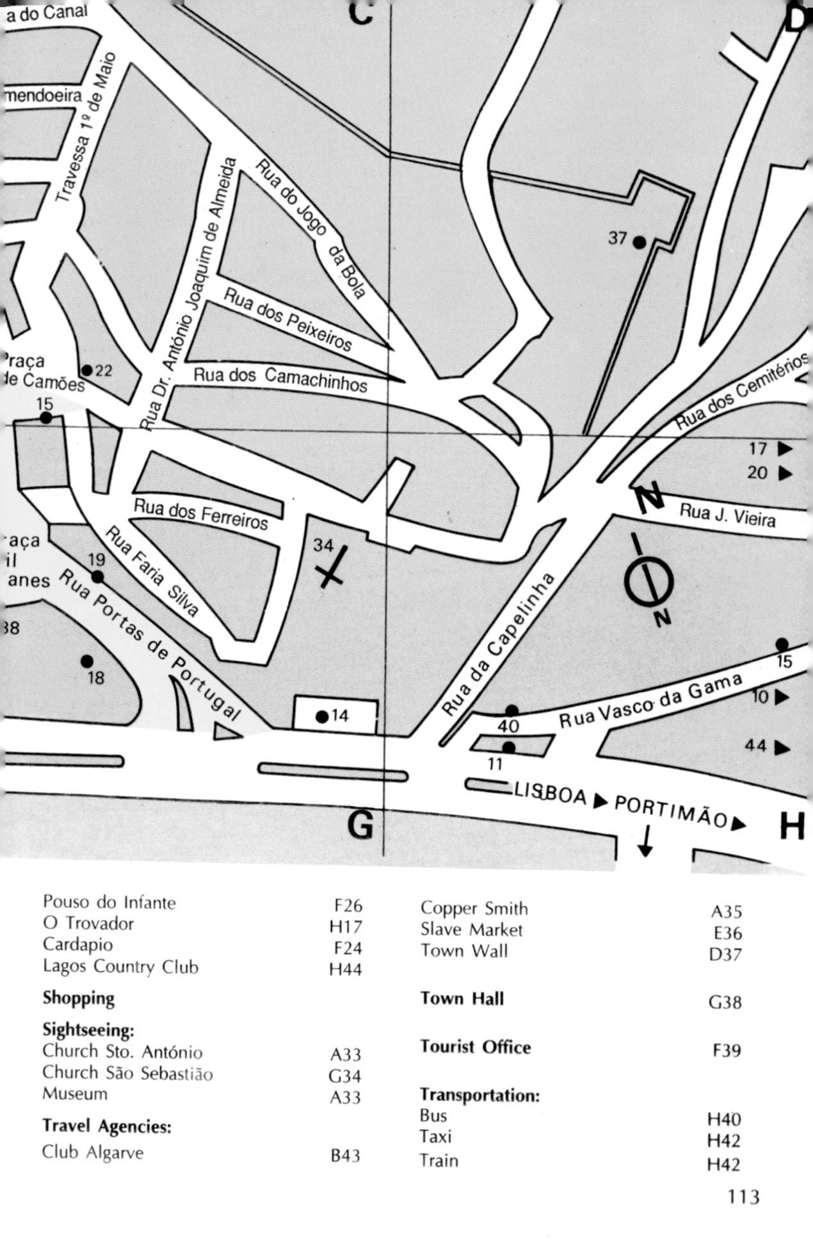

Pouso do Infante	F26
O Trovador	H17
Cardapio	F24
Lagos Country Club	H44

Shopping

Sightseeing:

Church Sto. António	A33
Church São Sebastião	G34
Museum	A33

Travel Agencies:

Club Algarve	B43
Copper Smith	A35
Slave Market	E36
Town Wall	D37

Town Hall G38

Tourist Office F39

Transportation:

Bus	H40
Taxi	H42
Train	H42

PONTA DA PIEDADE

Praia de D. Ana and Praia do Camilo are some of the beaches on the promontory lying to the south of Lagos. As they are so close to the town, they are easily accessible and well worth a day's sea and sun bathing. They are partly hidden by the high cliffs, but steps carved in the cliff faces make for reasonably easy access. For the more adventurous, there are old goat trails which may be followed as they wind their way from the cliff tops to the beaches below. One's day on the beach can alternate between basking in the sun or taking shelter from it in the cliff shadows. In season, one may take a snack at the beach huts which serve drinks and grilled sardines. One of the main sight-seeing places of the area is the **Ponta da Piedade**, some two kilometres south of Lagos. Here, flights of steps lead down to the sea and the rocks are riddled with natural arches and caves.

Praia do Camilo

Praia da Luz

Also alongside the road from **Lagos** to **Sagres** - some three kilometres from the highway - is the beautiful beach of **Praia da Luz**. Like so many other beaches along the Algarve coast, this area certainly has great and picturesque charm. There are many villas and apartments for rent here, and all are furnished to a high standard.

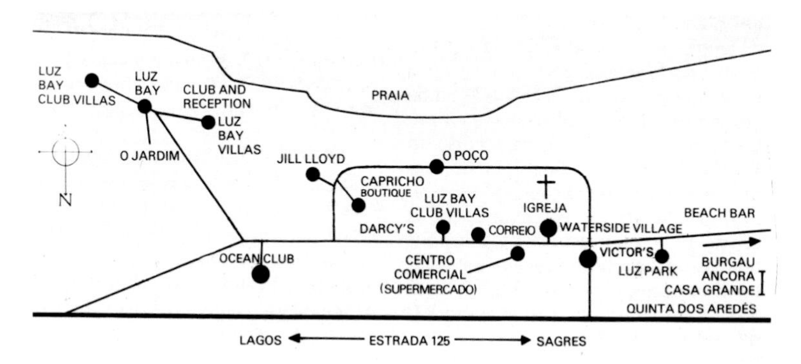

LUZ BAY has another attraction; the **Sea Sports Centre** run by **Detlef Seeger,** a German deep sea diving expert. Nine years ago he started the Sea Sports Club and now runs a very successful diving centre. Diving off the Portuguese coast is a sports option that very few visitors are aware of and yet the coral reefs and clear blue waters of the Atlantic are an underwater paradise. Other favourite dive spots are the caves of Ponta da Piedade, and two old sunken wrecks along the coast.

Underwater, the best scenic dives take place in ten to twenty metres of depth, often only minutes away from the shore. In the summer Detlef organises 2 dives a day, and a third, the night dive — on Fridays. All the necessary equipment can be rented from the centre. To reach the dive site, he uses 3 colourful traditional fishing boats, each fully equipped. Detlef is an expert at preparing the dive party, and making sure all participants are properly kitted-out. For more information contact Detlef Seeger, Sea Sports Centre, Av. dos Pescadores 4, Praia da Luz. Tel: (082) 789538. The centre also offers snorkelling, windsurfing, sailing, rowing and fishing and picnic boat trips.

There is also the **Ocean Club Watersports School**, which is run from a prime position on the beach at Praia da Luz a few minutes walk from the Ocean Club apartments. They specialise in windsurfing and sailing lessons and practice, since the beach offers near perfect conditions. All equipment is provided. You can also book watersports holidays at the school directly through its London headquarters at 30-32 Thames Street Kingston-upon-Thames Surrey KTI IPE. Tel (01) 5473406.

Accommodation

BEACH VILLAS OF CAMBRIDGE — Offering converted fishermen's cottages and villas with private swimming pools. For information/brochure, contact: Beach Villas Ltd 8 Market Passage, Cambridge, CB2 3QR, Tel. (0223) 311113, or Luz Tel. 789401.

See also page 117.

Restaurants — Bars

O JARDIM. At Luz Bay Club, open to all, set in spectacular sub-tropical gardens — cafeteria, full restaurant and lunch time snacks and salads. Charcoal grills a speciality in the evenings. Tel: 789555.

O POÇO. The beach bar at Praia da Luz located on the west side in front of the villas overlooking the beach. Easy parking. Al fresco dining. Open midmorning to late evening. Lunch time snacks. Fresh fish. Sardines a speciality.

BILLY'S - A restaurant providing excellent service and a top grade chef, extremely good food at reasonable prices. Also a typically portuguese outside cating area for light meals and refreshments. Take-away meals can be provided; only 100 metres from beach. Tel: (082) 789180, Rua da Praia n.º10.

O POÇO — Sr. Carlos, the proprietor is a seasoned caterer and knows how to care for his clients, and keep an eye on the action in the open kitchen. Very good Portuguese international cuisine and fresh fish. Warm atmosphere. Located **ALMADENA** Largo do Poço, 24. Tel: (082) 65433/65432.

THE OCEAN CLUB located in the village has its own beautiful club grounds and amenities. The privacy of the superb self-catering apartments combined with the hotel-like facilities cater to every wish of the holidaymaker. The apartments have each been finished with marble tiled bathrooms and Portuguese decorative tiled kitchens. All are privately owned and have been individually furnished to exceedingly high standards. Maid service is provided daily. See also page 116.

THE WATERSIDE VILLAGE. A well known architect, Robin Crosland, has beautifully designed the Waterside Village to blend with the old Luz village charm on what is one of Algarve's most dramatic beach locations. Owners are offered the choice of either 'on the beach' section of the village immediately overlooking the sea, or 'in the garden' section, attractively laid out and set around club gardens and pools. For information contact **THE OCEAN CLUB,** Praia da Luz, 8600 Lagos. Tel: (082) 789472. Telex: 57474 OCEANC P. Fax: (082) 789763.

BURGAU/SALEMA

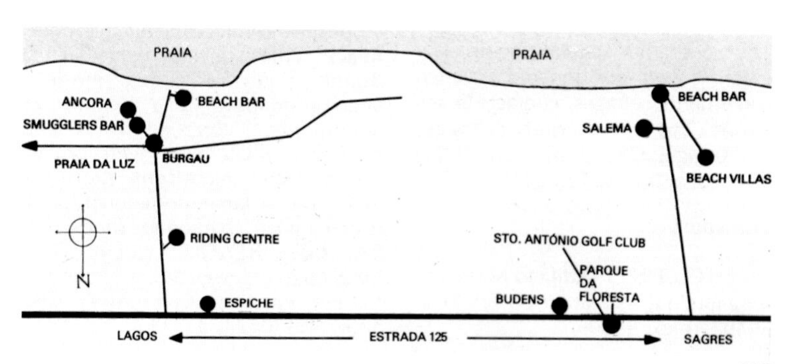

BURGAU - An unsophisticated but characterful village of multicoloured houses and narrow cobbled streets focusing on the village square and slipway. The houses are flanked by rocky slopes running down to a delightful golden beach. Some new development has added to the village amenities. Residents and visitors can now enjoy tennis, squash and a variety of other sports and recreational activities.

Accommodation

BEACH VILLAS OF CAMBRIDGE - Tour operators specialising in self-catering well-positioned converted fishermen's cottages, contact: Beach Villas Ltd, 8 Market Passage, Cambridge, CB2 3QR, Tel. (0223) 311113, or Burgau Tel. 69104.

Transport

AUTO CERRO - Edifício Marretas Burgau. 8650 Vila do Bispo Tel: (082) 69497 Telex: 57699.

Restaurants - Bars

ANCORA. Located in one of the picturesque cliff/beach areas overlooking the sea. Specialities include locally caught fish and lobster. Good food. Tel: 69102.

SMUGGLERS BAR For drinks, snacks - A super rendezvous! Full of colour and interest. Located on road to beach. Open 11 am until late. On Thurs. open at 7 pm.

BEACH BAR. For years Ralph and Keith have had the most popular bar-restaurant on the beach. Special steaks and locally caught fish are charcoal grilled (children's portions). Bar open daily 10.00-24.00 Restaurant 12.00-15.00 1900-22.00. For hire there are paddle boats, canoes, windsurfers, water skiing, sunshades and deck chairs. Tel: 60218.

SALEMA a fishing village nestling on green slopes leading down to a superb wide beach stretching for some 600 metres. The village has a few shops satisfying basic needs and a small number of bars and restaurants. Opposite the village the relatively new **Beach Villas** development Salema Beach Club provides modern accommodation in a mixture of apartments, terraced villas and detached villas most with private pools, plus excellent facilities including a large communal pool, restaurant/bar, barbeque, shops, etc. SALEMA BEACH CLUB Tel: (082) 65252. Beach Villas Limited, 8 Market Passage, Cambridge, CB2 3 QR, Tel (0223) 311113.

As one travels westwards past Lagos the landscape becomes harder and harsher. At **Sagres**, a small port on the southern side of **Cape St. Vincent**, Prince Henry the Navigator trained his captains and from there they set out to explore the world. He was Grand Master of the Order of Christ under whose flag (a red cross on a white background) the caravels sailed. Vasco da Gama and Christopher Columbus learned their skills here, though little remains to tell the modern visitor. The fortress of Sagres was rebuilt in the seventeenth century and one may see the old School of Seamanship within its walls. A giant compass (the famous 'Compass Rose') has been laid out in stones and it is said that Henry used this for his calculations. His house and the Graça chapel are also to be seen. The Ponta de Sagres commands breathtaking views over the sea and the coastline as far as Lagos. As the road takes you close to the edge of the cliffs there is a thrilling view of the sea pounding away hundreds of feet below. As this is also the principal lobster fishing area for the Algarve, one may also see the lobster boats making their way back to their port, the Bay of Sagres, where a new well protected harbour is being built.

Accommodation

HOTEL DA BALEEIRA (***) is beautifully located on a cove with a sandy beach. 120 comfortable rooms with private bath, telephone, central heating and all facing the sea. Amenities include TV room, discotheque, tennis court and a beautiful sea water swimming pool. Tel. 64212/3/4. Telex 57467 P. Fax: 64425

POUSADA DO INFANTE. (An official Portuguese inn - Class 1A). Well located, looking out over the coast. Has rooms with private bath and balcony, large dining room with sea front terrace. Tel. 64222/3.

SAGRES - CAPE ST. VINCENT

Accommodation

MOTEL GAMBOZINOS (***) Located just off the beach of Martinhal in a beautiful setting with no construction nearby. 17 rooms, some with sitting room. Doubles are the largest and some of the best in the area at reasonable prices. Informal service with a friendly staff that cares. The restaurant is closed on Wednesdays and in winter months November until February. Tel: (082) 64318/64348.

Restaurants

A TASCA, Whilst in Sagres do not miss this typical fishermen's bar/ restaurant with its breathtaking view overlooking the Bay of Baleeira. Professionally run - the best of Portuguese cuisine, fish straight from the sea. Live lobsters and crabs are kept in special salt water tanks. The atmosphere is friendly and the 'sea shore' decor interesting. Moderate prices. Tel. 64177

Sports

Fishing A fishing boat complete with all tackle and bait, for four persons can be hired by the day. **Sagres** and **Carrapateira** (16 kilometres to the north) and the beach of **Monte dos Clérigos** and **Arrifana** are considered by sportsmen to be the best fishing grounds in Portugal and among the best in Europe.

'O Fim do Mundo' - The end of the world. That is the name given to **Cape St. Vincent** by sailors long centuries ago. it is unquestionably one of the grandest geographical features in Europe, being the tip of the continent

which first meets the force of the raging Atlantic. Seas are always rough here and there is always a constant flow of shipping rounding the Cape. According to tradition it gets its name because the body of St. Vincent floated ashore here after his death at Valencia. Great naval battles have been fought here too. In 1693 a French fleet defeated the British and Dutch, while in 1770 the British gained victory over the Spaniards. In 1797 a British fleet led by Nelson and Jarvis defeated the French.

A tour of the **lighthouse** is a must. The light itself is the strongest in all Europe, throwing a beam sixty miles out to sea. A strange sight to observe as one drives very close to the cliffs are the local fishermen casting their long lines out over the cliff edge.

Situated nine kilometres from Faro **Olhão** is very like a North African town, for the houses and the church are built in the shape of white cubes, sometimes two or three storeys high. Unlike many towns and villages along the Algarve, Olhão's style owes nothing to the influence of Moorish conquerors, but is the result of modern trading links between its merchants and those of the North African coasts, similar buildings being found in Tunisia and Libya. The old part of the city is most attractive, although surrounded by more recent buildings. Though a fish market is held regularly, and boats are to be seen in the port, this activity is nothing like as important as in the past.

Sports. Fishing (angling and underwater), swimming, on the island of Armona close by.

Accommodation

HOTEL RIA-SOL (***) Olhão now has a comfortable hotel with 52 rooms all with bath, a bar and lounge. Rua General Humberto Delgado, 37. Tel: 72167. Telex: 56923 RISOL P.

QUINTA PALMEIRAS GARDEN CENTRE

The best one in the Algarve in fact! And what a glorious place -scene of thousands of palm trees, exotic flowers, plants and seedlings for gardens, homes, rockeries and pools. A walk through the warm, sticky greenhouses to see spectacular Hibiscus, Passion Flowers, Bouganvillea... Do visit beautiful Quinta Palmeiras where Eva and Detlev Von Rosen have created a well-known beautiful garden centre. Situated on EN 125 between Olhão and Tavira. Tel. (081) 96189.

Quinta Palmeiras

TAVIRA (32 Kms from Faro Airport)

Lying at the mouth of the **Ribeira da Asseca, Tavira** is said to be the most picturesque town in the Algarve. Though tunny and sardine fishing still provide employment, its harbour has been silted up and the town is cut off from the sea by a long spit of land. From the castle on the west bank there is a fine view of the town. At **Santa Luzia** , one kilometre to the south there is an excellent beach, and the beach at **Ilha de Tavira,** on the land between the town and the sea, is also popular. Tavira itself has two interesting churches. The church of the Misericordia has a fine Renaissance doorway and in the eighteenth century church of Santa Maria do Costrelo is the tomb of D. Paio Correia, liberator of the Algarve.

Restaurants - Bars

BEIRA RIO BARS AND RESTAURANT

An old riverside warehouse interestingly converted on two floors. The ground floor has restaurant and bars serving international and italian food with an additional cocktail Bar for your pleasure. The second floor was converted into a snooker room with bar and chinese restaurant with seating inside and out, overlooking the river. Rua Borda D'Água da Asseca, 46-48. Directly on the river Gílão 100 meters from the market place on the opposite bank. Tel: (081) 23165.

Accommodation

QUINTA DE PEROGIL.

Perched above the town of Tavira, Quinta de Perogil offers a spectacular site for your 3, 4 or 5 bedroomed villa. The 23 hectares are filled with old fruit trees, and apartments, a sports center and shops are also planned. The view down to the beaches and sea is spectacular. Contact them at Rua Jacques Pessoa, 15 - 8800 Tavira. Tel: (081) 22145. Telex: 56080.

EUROTEL TAVIRA (***), Member of Eurotel International Chain. 80 rooms offering every comfort. Full bath, mini-bar, telephone, radio, balcony overlooking sea or hills. Amenities include restaurant, bar, swimming pool, tennis courts, mini-golf, table tennis, children's playground, open disco, TV room. Located in the countryside on the main road between Cabanas/Tavira, within easy reach of beach. Tel: (081) 22041. Telex: 56218.

EUROTEL ALTURA (***), Member of Eurotel International Chain. 135 rooms facing the sea, offering every comfort. Full bath, balcony, mini-bar, radio and telephone. Amenities: restaurant, bar, indoor and outdoor swimming pool, tennis courts, mini-golf, private beach facilities, children's playground, disco, TV room, table tennis, shops. Located on beach between Monte Gordo/ Tavira. Tel: (081) 95450. Telex: 56068.

PEDRAS D'EL REI Holiday villages have a total of 4632 beds distributed in apartments and villas ranging from type "TO" to "V4". In this way both complexes can offer accommodation to suit all styles from a simple studio to a villa for groups or large families. The large number of holiday beds in these villages is backed up by all the infrastructures and communal services which are essential to ensure that your holidays will be as easy and trouble free as possible. ST.ª LUZIA Tel. (081) 22176/7 Telex: 56044 CABANAS Tel (081) 20181/2. Telex: 56012.

ALJEZUR Algarve's West Coast (108 kms from Faro Airport)

In the general area of the small town of Aljezur there are wide open spaces offering panoramic views of land and sea. There are sandy unspoiled beaches and large green spaces of pinewood and grassland. The tranquility is disturbed only by birds and other small creatures. The beaches that are accessible and have some facilities are - **Odeceixe, Amoreira, Monte Clérigo** and **Arrifana**. There are side trips through small hamlets and to historical sites fo be taken. **Restaurant: Vale da Telha**. Main restaurant in the area, Portuguese cooking, a pleasant rustic setting. Tel. 72180: **Accommodation**: **Hotel Vale da Telha** (****), Residential, 26 rooms all with private bath. Tel. 72180/5. Telex 57466. Both located at Vale de Telha 5 miles from town.

S. BRÁS DE ALPORTEL (24 kms from Faro Airport)

North east of Loulé, set high over magnificent scenery is the charming village of S. Brás de Alportel. It has a Pousada.

Accommodation

POUSADA DE S. BRÁS (Class 1A). 21 rooms, 18 with private bath. Good Portuguese cooking with regional specialities. Very pleasant. Reservations: Tel. 42305.

FUSETA

Six miles farther east, this is somewhat similar to Olhão, but on a smaller scale.

MILREU-ESTOI

Close to route N2, where a minor road branches from it to the village of Estoi, are the Roman and early Christian remains of **Milréu**. Little has been done to preserve them since their discovery in 1876 but one can see the remains of Roman baths, some attractive mosaics and fragments of columns. The ancient name of the site was Ossonoba and a building there is said to be a third century Christian church. If so, it is one of the earliest in the world. Close by the palace and formal park and fountains of **Estoi** are worth visiting. The gardens contain statues and mosaics from the Milreu site.

Near the mouth of the river **Guadiana**, this is one of the most delightful and unusual beaches in the entire province. Here, at **Praia de Monte Gordo,** the pine trees reach down to the pale gold sands at the water's edge. It has developed considerably as a holiday resort, and the town itself is attractive.

Among excursions which may be enjoyed from Monte Gordo is a visit to **Vila Nova de Cacela,** just five kilometres away, with its quiet lovely beach and wooded shore. **Castro Marim**, nearby, has the remains of a castle founded by Afonso II and from there one may enjoy views of the coast, the hills of Spain and the Guadiana valley.

On two hills nearby are the church of Nossa Senhora dos Mártires and the fort of San Sebastião.

Hotel Vasco da Gama

HOTEL VASCO DA GAMA (****) The only hotel located on Monte Gordo's sandy beach. 200 rooms and suites, all with private bathroom, telephone and music. Restaurant, Bar, Nightclub — 2 swimming pools (adults and children) with Snackbar. 4 tennis courts (2 floodlit), Minigolf, Bowling, Table-Tennis. Private beach with Restaurant — water skiing and windsurfing. Colour TV Room. Bridge and Reading Room. Located Av. Infante D. Henrique, 8900 Monte Gordo. Tel. (081) 44321. Telex 56020. VAGAMA P.

HOTEL DOS NAVEGADORES (***) 346 rooms, all with private bath, telephone and central heating. Also restaurant, bar, spacious lobby, covered pool, a Health Club (with squash, sauna, gymnasium, jacuzzi, Turkish bath, Scottish bath, massage) and a conference room for 150 people. Also visit the snack bar on beach, the Dom Jotta bar-restaurant at Ponta de Stº António and the Copacabana bar-restaurant on the main avenue. Tel: (081) 42490 Fax: (081) 44872. Telex: 56054.

Pool at "Hotel dos Navegadores"

Accommodation

Aparthotel Atlântico

APARTHOTEL ATLÂNTICO (***) Recently opened. 88 apartments beautifully located with balconies overlooking beach. Fully furnished for self-catering. Room temperature controls. Avenida Infante Henrique. Tel: 44040. Telex: 56290 Fax: 44872.

ALBERGARIA MONTE GORDO (****) American operated, 49 rooms all with private bath, most with balcony, overlooking extensive beach. Outstanding food in beach view restaurant and attractive bar with music, open to the public. Special off season rates Tel. 42124 Cable Montotel.

Accommodation (continued)

HOTEL ALCAZAR (****) 95 rooms and suites, all fully air conditioned, private bathroom, radio and telephone. Also has a swimming pool. Tel. 42184/6. Cable Hotalcasar-Monte Gordo Telex 56028.

Transport

AVIS. Rua Gil Eanes, 6-A, Tel. 44554. Telex 56737 P.

BUDGET RENT-A-CAR - Apartamentos Montesol, Rua 10, Lote 1 Tel. 44027 Telex. 56019.

EUROPCAR INTERNATIONAL — Praça Luís de Camões, Loja D. Tel.: 41747 Fax: 41748.

Vila Real de Santo António

Castro Marim

This town on the bank of the **Guadiana** river marks Portugal's frontier with Spain and car and pedestrian ferries run a regular service across the river to **Ayamonte** on the Spanish side. The town was founded in 1774 on the site of an earlier town which had been engulfed by sea and sand. Because of its comparatively recent foundation, it is the only town in the Algarve where all the streets are laid out straight on a grid pattern.

Sightseeing. It is interesting to cross the river by ferry and see the Spanish side and the city of Ayamonte.

Accommodation

HOTEL APOLO. Recently built. 42 rooms, all with private bath and balcony. The bar is most attractive and comfortable. A restaurant with national and regional dishes. Excellent for seaside holidays and water sports - but also when simply visiting the area or travelling into Spain. Located in front of the voluntary Fire Station. Tel: (081) 44448/9. Telex: 56902 P.

Shopping.

Blocked off to traffic, the shopping promenade is interesting to walk along looking for good buys and souvenirs. When tired, rest at one of the sidewalk cafes.

Restaurants

CAVES DO GUADIANA. Portuguese operated. Located on main street facing ferry docks. Specialities, seafood and Portuguese cuisine. Av. da Republica, 89. Tel: 44498.

MANUEL D'ÁGUA. Near the Castro Marim Fort walls and overlooking river-marshes, this down-to-earth eating spot is one of the best for grilled fish. Tel: (081) 43880.

General information on ferries to Spain: There is a ferry approximately every 1/2 hour. **Running hours:** November 1st to March 31st - 07.00 to 23.00 April 1st to October 31st - 07.00 to 23.00. **Passage fare:** Car 600$00 and for each person 100$00.

Where to Stay

¥ **Conference Facilities**

	HOTELS	Rating	Location	Page
	Avenida Praia	***	Praia da Rocha	101
	Albacor	**	Faro	56
	Alcazar	****	Monte Gordo	126
¥	**Alfamar**	*****	Falésia	74
¥	**Algarve**	*****	Praia da Rocha	102
	Almansor	****	Carvoeiro	90
	Apolo	**	Vila Real de Santo António	127
¥	**Alvor Praia**	*****	Praia dos Três Irmãos	106
	Atlantis - Vilamoura	*****	Vilamoura	72
¥	**Balaia**	*****	Albufeira	79
	Baleeira	****	Sagres	119
	Boa Vista	****	Albufeira	78
	Cerro Alagoa	****	Albufeira	79
	Da Aldeia	***	Albufeira	78
	Delfim	****	Praia dos Três Irmãos	106
	Dona Filipa	*****	Vale do Lobo	66
¥	**Dom João**	*****	Alvor Praia	107
	Dom José	***	Quarteira	70
	Dom Pedro Golf	****	Vilamoura	71
	Dom Pedro Portobelo	****	Vilamoura	71
	Dom Pedro Marina	****	Vilamoura	71
	Dom Sancho	****	Carvoeiro	90
¥	**Eva**	*****	Faro	55
	Faro	***	Faro	56
	Garbe	****	Armação de Pêra	87
¥	**Golfinho**	****	Praia Dos Três Irmãos	107
	Jupiter	****	Praia da Rocha	101
	Levante	****	Armação de Pêra	107
	Meia Praia	****	Meia Praia	110
¥	**Montechoro**	****	Albufeira	77
	Navegadores	***	Monte Gordo	125
	Oriental	****	Praia da Rocha	102
¥	**Penina**	*****	Penina	108
	Quinta do Lago	*****	Quinta do Lago	65
	Vasco de Gama	****	Monte Gordo	125
	Vilamoura Marinotel	*****	Vilamoura	72

Where to Eat

(Gastronomy - pages 18 and 19)

LANGUAGE GUIDE

ARRIVAL IN PORTUGAL I am coming **Venho**, on holiday **de ferias**, on business **em viagem de negócios**. My passport **O meu passaporte**, ticket **bilhete**, visa **visto.** One suitcase is missing **Falta uma mala** I have **Tenho**, nothing to declare **nada a declarar** What is the best way to get from here to...? **Qual o melhor caminho para...?** Please call a taxi **Chame-me um taxi por favor** My luggage is **A minha bagagem está**, in the hold **no porão**, in the guard's van, **no vagão do comboio,** here **aqui**.

ASKING DIRECTIONS Is this right for...? **Vou bem para?** Can you direct me to...**Pode indicar-me o caminho para...,** the railway station **a estação**, the Underground **o Metro**, the police station **o posto da policia**, a garage **uma garagem**, a phone box **uma cabine telefonica**, a doctor **um médico**, the centre of the city, **o centro da cidade**, the way out of the city to...**a saída da cidade para...,** a good hotel **um bom hotel**.

CHEMIST A bandage **uma ligadura**, cotton-wool **algodão**, sticking plaster **adesivos**, aspirin **aspirina**, a toothbrush **escova de dentes**, talcum powder **pó de talco** Have you anything for...? **O que tem para...** colds **constipações**, bad sunburn **queimaduras de sol**, constipation **prisão de ventre**, diarrhoea **diarreia**, sore feet **pés doridos**, toothache **dor de dentes**, corns **calos**, headache **dor de cabeça**, sore throat **dor de garganta**.

COLOURS White **Branco**, black **preto**, red **encarnado**, blue **azul**, green **verde**, brown **castanho**, yellow **amarelo**, pink **cor de rosa**, grey **cinzento**, dark **escuro**, light **claro**.

COMMON PHRASES Please help me **Ajude-me por favor** Please tell me **Informe-me por favor** Please dial this number and call **Por favor marque este numero e chame...** What is the address? **Qual o endereco?** What is the phone number? **Qual o número de telefone?** How much is it? **Quanto custa?** Send for **Mande chamar**, a doctor **um médico** Where is the toilet? **Onde ficam os lavabos?** I don't feel well **Sinto-me mal disposta** I am **Tenho**, hungry **fome,** thirsty **sede**, in a hurry **pressa** Why? **Porquê?** Where? **Onde?**

DAYS, MONTHS, SEASONS Sun. **Domingo**, Mon. **Segunda-feira**, Tues. **Terça-feira**, Wed. **Quarta-feira**, Thurs, **Quinta-feira**, Fri. **Sexta-feira**, Sat. **Sábado** January **Janeiro**, February **Fevereiro**, March **Março**, April **Abril**, May **Maio**, June **Junho**, July **Julho**, August **Agosto**, Sept. **Setembro** Oct. **Outubro**, Nov. **Novembro**, Dec. **Dezembro** Spring **Primavera**, Summer **Verão**, Autumn **Outono**, Winter **Inverno.**

GREETINGS ETC. Good morning **Bom dia** Good afternoon or evening **Boa tarde** Goodnight **Boa noite**/Good bye **Adeus**/So long **Até logo**/Yes **Sim**/ No **Não**/Please **Por favor**/Thank you **Muito obrigado**/Excuse me **Com licença**/I am sorry **Desculpe.**

HOTEL A single room **Um quarto simples,** a double room **um quarto de casal,** with private bathroom **com banho**, full board **pensão completa**, bed and breakfast **quarto e pequeno almoço**/Call **Chame**, the manager **o gerente**/Bring me **Traga-me,** a towel **uma toalha**, soap **sabonete**, toilet paper **papel higiénico**, mineral water **água mineral**/Is there any mail? **Há correspondência**/Please keep this for me **guarde-me isto por favor**.

KIOSKS Have you **Vendem**, films for this camera **filmes para esta máquina,** newspapers **jornais**, books **livros**, magazines **revistas**, in English **em inglês**, writing-paper **papel de carta**, cigarettes **cigarros**, cigars **charutos**, pipe tobacco **tabaco para cachimbo**, matches **fósforos**, ballpoint pens **esferográficas**, postcards **postais**, sunglasses **óculos de sol**, special stamps **selos especiais?**

MEASUREMENTS Big **Grande**, Bigger **Maior**, Small **Pequeno**, Smaller **Mais pequeno**, Wide **Largo**, Tight **Apertado**, Long **Comprido**, Short **Curto**, Round **Redondo**, Square **Quadrado**, Thick **Espesso**, Thin **Fino**.

MONEY How much have I to pay? **Quanto tenho a pagar?** Do you take traveller's cheques? **Aceitam "travellers" cheques?** Can I have **Pode dar-me?** the bill **a conta**, the receipt **o recibo**, the change **o troco**, Can I pay **Posso pagar** in foreign currency **com moeda estrangeira**, Can you change? **Pode trocar?** A bank **Um banco**, What is the rate of exchange **Qual é o câmbio?** Signature **Assinatura** Notes **Notas** Coins **Moedas**.

NUMBERS 1 **um**, 2 **dois**, 3 **três**, 4 **quatro**, 5 **cinco**, 6 **seis**, 7 **sete**, 8 **oito**,

9 **nove**, 10 **dez**, 11 **onze**, 12 **doze**, 13 **treze**, 14 **catorze**, 15 **quinze**, 16 **dezasseis**, 17 **dezassete**, 18 **dezoito**, 19 **dezanove**, 20 **vinte**, 21 **vinte e um**, 30 **trinta**, 40 **quarenta**, 50 **cinquenta**, 60 **sessenta**, 70 **setenta**, 80 **oitenta**, 90 **noventa**, 100 **cem**, 101 **cento e um**, 1000 **mil**, 1001 **mil e um**.

POST OFFICE What is the postage? **Quanto e a franquia**, on this letter **nesta carta**, postcard **bilhete postal**, parcel **volume**, by air mail **por via aérea**, by registered post **registado**, Iwant to send a cable to...**Quero mandar um telegrama para...**Stamps **Selos**, Postal order **Vale de correio**.

RESTAURANT The menu **A ementa**, Breakfast **Pequeno almoço**, Lunch **almoço**, Dinner **Jantar**, Tea **Lanche,** Head waiter **Chefe de mesa**, The bill **a conta**, Is the service included?**O serviço está incluido?** The wine list **A lista dos vinhos**.

SHOPPING Shop **Uma loja**, Shoe-shop **Sapataria**, Jeweller's **Joalharia**, Stationer's **Papelaria**, Handicrafts shop **Artesanato**, Souvenirs **Lembranças**, Market **Mercado**, Baker's **Padaria**, Butcher's **Talho**, Supermarket , **Supermercado**, Grocer's **Mercearia**, Fishmonger's **Peixaria,** 'A pound (weight) **Meio quilo**, **Material** (cloth) **Fazenda**, Dress **Vestido**, Skirt **Saia**, Suit **Fato**, Blouse **Blusa**, Shirt **Camisa**, Stockings **Meias**, Raincoat **Gabardine**, Handkerchief **Lenço**, Shoes **Sapatos**, Bathing suit **Fato de banho**, Sunglasses **Óculos de sol**, Tablecloth **Toalha de mesa**, Towel **Toalha**, Glazed Tiles **Azulejos**, Necklace **Colar**, Belt **Cinto,** Necktie **Gravata**, Silk **Seda**, Cotton **Algodão,** Linen **Linho**, Wool **Lã**, Expensive **Caro**, Cheap **Barato**.

SIGHTSEEING Town **Cidade**, Little town **Vila**, Village **Aldeia**, Museum **Museu**, Church **Igreja**, Old part of the town **Cidade antiga**, Castle **Castelo**, Guide **Guia**, Interpreter **Interprete**, Entrance ticket **Bilhete de entrada**, Way in **Entrada**, Way out **Saida**.

TIME What time is it? **Que horas são**? When **Quando**, do you open? **abrem?** shut? **fecham?**, When will it be ready? **Quando fica pronto?**, Immediately **Imediatamente,** Very soon **Logo**, Tomorrow **Amanhã,** Today **Hoje**, This afternoon **Logo a tarde**, This evening **Logo a noite**, Yesterday **Ontem**, The day after tomorrow **Depois de amanhã,** The day before yesterday **Anteontem**, Late **Tarde**, Early **Cedo**, One day **Um dia**, One night **Uma noite**, Midday **Meio dia**, Midnight **Meia noite**.

FOOD GUIDE

How to order coffee: **Bica** - A small, black coffee, **Galão** - a glass of white coffee, **Garoto** - a cup of white coffee, **Meia de Leite** - a large cup of white coffee, **Carioca** - A small cup of coffee diluted with hot water

AVES DE CAÇA *POULTRY/GAME*

Codorniz .... Quail
Coelho .... Rabbit
Frango .... Chicken
Galinha .... Hen
Pato .... Duck
Perdiz .... Partridge
Peru .... Turkey

CARNE—*MEAT*

Borrego .... Lamb
Bife .... Steak
Cabrito .... Kid
Carneiro .... Mutton
Entrecosto .... Rumpsteak
Escalope .... Escalope
Fiambre .... Ham
Fígado .... Liver
Leitão .... Sucklingpig
Língua .... Tongue
Lombo .... Fillet
Porto .... Pork
Rins .... Kidneys
Bacon .... Bacon
Vaca .... Beef
Vitela .... Veal

FRUTAS—*FRUIT*

Alperces .... Apricots
Ameixas .... Plums
Amêndoas .... Almonds
Amendoim .... Peanuts
Ananás .... Pineapple
Avelãs .... Hazlenuts
Bananas .... Bananas
Figos .... Figs
Framboesas .. Raspberries
Laranja .... Orange
Limão .... Lemon
Maçã .... Apple
Melão .... Melon
Morango .... Strawberry
Pera .... Pear
Pêssego .... Peach
Toranja .... Grapefruit
Uvas .... Grapes

LEGUMES—*VEGETABLES*

Abóbora .... Pumpkin
Agriões .... Watercress
Alcachofras .... Artichokes
Alho .... Garlic
Arroz .... Rice
Batatas .... Potatoes
Beringelas .... Egg-plant
Cebolas .... Onions
Cenouras .... Carrots
Cogumelos .... Mushrooms
Couve .... Cabbage
Couve-flor ...... Cauliflower
Ervilhas .... Green peas
Espargos .... Asparagus
Espinafres .... Spinach
Favas .... Broad Beans
Feijão .... Beans
Lentilhas .... Lentils
Nabos .... Turnips
Pepino .... Cucumber
Pimentos .... Peppers
Rabanetes .... Radishes
Salsa .... Parsley

MARISCOS—*SHELLFISH*

Amêijoas .... Clams
Camarões .... Shrimps
Caranguejos .... Crabs
Gambas .... Prawns
Lagosta .... Rock Lobster
Lagostins .... Crayfish
Lavagante .... Lobster
Lulas .... Squid
Mexilhões .... Mussels
Ostras .... Oysters
Perceves .... Barnacles
Polvo .... Octopus
Santola .... Big crabs
Chocos .... Cuttlefish
Vieiras .... Scallops

OVOS—*EGGS* ....

Cozidos .... Hardboiled
Escalfados .... Poached
Estrelados .... Fried
Mexidos .... Scrambled
Omoleta .... Omelet
Quentes .... Boiled

PEIXE—*FISH* ....

Atum .... Tuna
Bacalhau .... Cod
Carpa .... Carp
Cherne .... Turbot
Eirós .... Sea eel
Espadarte .... Swordfish
Linguado .... Sole
Pargo .... Bream
Peixe-Espada Scabbardfish
Pescada .... Hake
Solha .... Plaice
Raia .... Skate
Robalo .... Sea bass
Salmonete .... Red mullet
Carapau .... Mackerel
Sardinhas .... Sardines
Savel .... Shad
Salmão .... Salmon
Truta .... Trout

PREPARO—*COOKING*

Assado .... Roasted
Corado .... Browned
Cozido .... Boiled
Bem passado .... Well done
Mal passado .... Rare
Médio .... Medium
Empada .... Pie
Estufado .... Stewed
Frito .... Fried
Fumado .... Smoked
Grelhado .... Grilled
Guisado .... Stew
Nas brasas .... Braised
No Espeto .... On the spit
No forno .... Baked
Manteiga .... Butter
Gelo .... Ice
Pimenta .... Pepper
Sal .... Salt
Azeite .... Olive oil
Vinagre .... Vinegar

WINE TERMS

Vinho branco white wine
Vinho clarete .... light red wine
Vinho consumo .... ordinary wine
Vinho de mesa .... table wine
Vinho engarrafado bottled wine
Vinho espumante sparkling wine
Vinho garrafeira a wine of exceptional quality harvest
Vinho reserva .... a selected wine of a good year
Vinho rosado ...... rosé wine
Vinho tinto .... red wine

Try
all
the
Frank
Cook
guides !
Costa Verde
Costa Verde
Costa Verde
Madeira
Costa Verde
Lisbon
Algarve